FOREWORD

Welcome to the third volume in a series by and for Benicia's "First Tuesday Poets" and friends. This anthology has been eagerly awaited by many whose work is in its pages. Each poet's work has been matched with a visual image illustrative of at least one of the associated poems.

This project is a continuum of a series started by our first Poet Laureate of Benicia, Joel Fallon. It was he who brought First Tuesday Poets into existence and started making things happen. Now as our first Poet Laureate Emeritus, Fallon continues to be a source of aid, influence and inspiration to our group.

We would like to extend our earnest appreciation to the Benicia Public Library for giving the First Tuesday Poets a home, and to the Benicia Historical Museum for hosting the group on several occasions.

Please join us on the "First Tuesday" of every month for a delightful evening of poetry. Check with the library for current dates and times.

Good cheer, poets and readers. Enjoy!

Robert M. Shelby.

Poet Laureate, Benicia
2008 - 2010

Acknowledgements:

I wish to thank Joel Fallon and Robert M. Shelby who
encouraged this project; Ronna Leon, who graciously shared her
photos; Sherry Sheehan for her invaluable proofreading skills;
and the poets for their unending patience.

Carole Dwinell
— *editor/publisher, Windows & Skylights*

TABLE OF CONTENTS

TAMRA
JANE
AMATO

DINOSAURS ARE NOT EXTINCT,
ONE LIVES IN MY HOUSE
(for Colin)

A contemporary creature,
this Tyrannosaurus Rex is not a carnivore.
He delights in gnashing peanut butter sandwiches
and his habitat is lush
with rocks and bugs and toys
and if I dare suggest he is a little boy —
his mighty roar is deafening.
Its echo captures ancient pains
that live in mother's heart
and for a moment
renders them extinct,
as joy tears them apart.

FRANK — FRIEND AND SPIRITUAL TEACHER

A holy man
in a hospital bed
preciously wrapped,
like a mystic infant —
radiant, beautifully sculpted
against white sheets.

You're dying you say.
Your voice a lamp,
another lesson strung
on a rosary of sacred moons,
to be held in prayer,
while darkness swaddles you.

EASTER IN SAN FRANCISCO, 1999

Our dreams begin to open on the ninth floor
of the Marines' Memorial Hotel.
Clean tombs equipped with all that is needed
for a weekend to die for and
guests view what they can see at their level.
Flags wave from rooftops of skyscrapers,
like spring flowers praising the high winds.
Below a jungle of souls
in hypnotic allegiance flow past
concrete fields choked with roads.
Fatigued, dormant dreams weakly climb
praying to continue, to go on,
hoping to recognize
silence as it sings a sacred invitation
to follow the fire of morning.
In our room we listen to the
television flicker between old graying movies
and a war in Kosovo.
At the window we have the luxury to turn away ...
and witness the massacre of our afternoon.
Hailstones bullet the sunlight,
day bleeds pools of darkness.
Night falls to the light
of colors resurrected in our hearts –
a sign flies triumphant,
emblazoned with life.
Who do you tell what your heart sees?
Who would believe the sound of it?

Oh Love, Oh Light —

"Please stay with us, for it is nearly evening and the day
  is almost over." — Luke 24:29

ON GRANDMA THORA'S FARM

I hide in Grandma Thora's room.
A velvet and wood reserve,
forbidden to children.
Grandma's heavy, hunting feet
thunder over hardwood floors toward me.
Curled up tight — like a snake,
praying my thumping chest doesn't climb
over her huge scolding voice,
and betray my hiding place.
Grandma Thora is in cahoots with God —
She is as scary as His commanding bible.
The book, that I didn't ask for, is my birthday gift.
I'm ashamed of my disappointment
that stepped into me when
I tore off the wrapping paper
and found only God's word.
King James in leather is not what I want.
I carve into the skin-thin title page
with a sharp tipped pen,
"Damn you! Go to Hell!"

God, I'm dead now for sure.

TAMRA JANE AMATO

FRANCES
ANDERSON-JACKSON

THE BATTLE AT TROSSEL'S HOUSE
Contrasting Two Daguerreotypes from the Civil War

Echos of a distant hell focus as one contemplates "The Halt"
Capturing the grim visage of war in the corpses of horses
    and men.
Have you ever loved horses? A soldier, far from home,
    weary and afraid
At the sight of Captain Page's good war steed at pasture
Might approach, place his arms around the sun warmed
    neck where
The smells of hay and musk would take him home - home
    as an ideal.

City dwellers in the hubs of industry kept an ideal of home too.
They worked and played there as children, not in fact, but in
    fiction.
On bridges, by rivers, in deep grass and crafted barns
    where
The weary soldier returns through the equine smells of
    flesh - to home..
I wonder the nature of man. Are hunters and agrarians
    distinct? Or are they both
In one man, his horse bound to the plow, but most idealized
    in battle?

How ironic these plates, side by side, grotesque and deflated
    glory
Next to the image of days when weapons are shelved and
Horses and men rest in pastoral peace which war's labor
    earned.
These dead surely knew courage. Or is it in our minds they
    are transformed
From corpse to martyr? I think they were partly brave
Partly mad, angry and frightened men who folded their
    courage about them

Like a cloak against the last journey and returned to earth.
continued next page

                                               FRANCES ANDERSON-JACKSON

Or, was just one stunned by a bitter flash of enlightenment
       like Melville,
For "What like a bullet can undeceive?" Those plunderers
       and users of equal flesh!
While they spoke or whispered in vainglorious voices - this
       multitude of
Wordless horses pitched and fell, their lifeblood mingling in
       the earth
Of a thousand battlefields, and here, at Trossel's House.

KARMA

God rules me with a mighty hand
And smites me with a karmic blow
That resonates and leaves me trembling
In palpable Belief
Until the next time, and the next, and the next...

THE ATHEIST

I'm blanketed over in weary days
That cover up poor little me
For I've lost a small thing with little brown eyes
That closed, and now I can't see.

I'm covered in layers of sorrowful days
My sheets are soaked in their grief.
Why me, why not me and back to why me
Where is this vague path to belief?

There's no God, that's assured - I always knew that
Still I promised Him promises kept.
Oh I'm blanketed over in wearisome days
And bargains that haven't been met.

From blankets that cover me over in days
Or maybe in weeks, I can't say
I nag and I rag at Who doesn't exist
But has carried my dearest away.

So what have I learned, that my sorrow has earned
Under blankets of pity for me?
It's that mercy is random and fairness a phantom
I'm finished with nights on my knees.

Oh I'm covered in blankets of bitters no doubt
And there's only me in the room
And it comes to me naggingly, draggingly slow
To vacate this bed pretty soon.

There's nothing else for it except to endure it.
My hand reaches out like a crone's.
I stand but not steady, because I'm not ready.
I'm bound to the Cross I disown.

FRANCES ANDERSON-JACKSON

A Legend in my own mind

PETER BRAY

EARLY AND LATE IN THE RIVER

1. *The Compost News Blues*

Rockets and vessels and algae stew,
these are the things that I once drew.
Didn't make Life nor the cover of Time,
but the Compost News had a cover of mine.

Ten thousand copies went through the mail,
a shower of glory or was it hail?
No Golden Record upon my wall
but the Compost News hangs there for all.

No, I didn't make Life nor the cover of Time,
but the Compost News ... thinks I'm divine.

2. *Berkeley October*

A Berkeley girlie with frosted cheek,
who looked my way though as not to speak.
And a campus gardener with hand held rigid,
numbed to the bone by water frigid,
that splashed to a concrete walk.
I came, I saw, and I went.

3. *You and Fyodor and Change*

You and Fyodor and change
came down to my place in the summer sun
and brought with you the nighttime
in all its splendid colors.
And it pulsed me through the evening
like some mammoth trucker's tailgate
hauling onions from San Josie
to the East Coast through the night.

— *continued next page*

PETER BRAY

4. *The Pebble That I Was*

She came to me as always
like the fragrance of a flower
and tucked between the pages
of my ignorance and my arrogance,
she chanced to read me and believe me
like the pages of a book.
And no words within my head
nor ever mumbled from my bed
shall sanctify the feelings
that I knew.
And the pebble that I was
soon became a castled rock.

5.*Pedro's On the Road to GO*

There's Peter, Paul, and Mary,
Tom, Dick, and Harry,
Curly, Moe, and Larry,
even Einstein is scary.
I had two years of high school Spanish
where they called me Pedro,
so like Huevos Rancheros,
I'm on the road to Go.

I've never been to Paris,
never been to Rome,
but I've been across the county line,
and I'm rarin' to go.
I had two years of high school Spanish
telling me all I know,
so like Huevos Rancheros,
I'm on the road to Go.

Some go by plane,
some go by train,

— *continued next page*

— *continued from previous page*

some folks you know,
they go by a single name.
There's Elvis and Madonna,
and Cher's another one too,
you can call me Pedro
if you've got nothin' else to do!

My money's in a sack,
tools are in the back.
Wanted Signs are posted
on both sides of the railroad tracks.
I had two years of high school Spanish,
telling me all I know,
so like Huevos Rancheros,
I'm on the road to Go.
Like Huevos Rancheros,
I'm on the road to Go.
I'm on the road to Go.

6. New Colors

When the economy hit the toilet
even the chameleons
were looking for new colors.
"I can speak in Blue and Green,"
said the first chameleon.
"I can make Lime Green
a whole new flavor sensation,"
said the second.
"But wait'll you see me dance
in Navajo White," said the third,
"you ain't seen nothing.
I can make the rain clouds form."
And with a clap of his own thunder
the third chameleon did his dance
in Navajo White and it rained
until his colors ran.

A WRITER'S CHALLENGE

To step into the space of a blank page,
        collage it with imaginary color.

To walk hand-in-hand with wonder,
        wrap souls with magical warmness.

To inhale the breezes of fantasy's breaths,
        create fabrications in the wind.

To embrace feelings of hidden meaning,
        to reap unearthed ideas.

To celebrate vivacious voices,
        release inhibitions from shy silence.

To seduce bare paper with passionate words,
        then to dare someone to read them.

REFLECTION

Waves embrace the sand,
    shiny sparkles smiling back,
        soothe a hurting heart.

WHEN ONE APPLE FALLS

The leaves of time transform
their colors more quickly
                    as we age.

You and I met in the
playful periods of our twenties,
fruitful in our ploys
to devour every
                    lush moment,

timeless, side-by-side
we blithely danced
                    through each season.

Now we find ourselves
like ripened skins mulched
            into a bed of soft knowledge.

Your arm looped through mine,
we marvel the apple orchard,
caress the crispness,
remember their round greenness,
as they turn
                    to gold and red,

know as one apple falls,
the other one
            will
                    eventually
                            follow.

BEAGLE LOVE

Those big brown eyes say it all.
When I look at her face,
unconditional approval
of my presence.

When I look at her face,
she gazes with admiration
of my presence,
just being together is enough.

She gazes with admiration,
fetching her favorite toy.
Just being together is enough,
no matter what the game.

Fetching her favorite toy,
moments warm and pleasant.
No matter what the game,
her companionship brings joy.

Moments warm and pleasant.
Time to frolic and play,
her companionship brings joy
Those big brown eyes say it all.

CHUCK
CONNER

THROUGH A WHITE WINDOW

Ragged white curtains rippling in the breeze
with yellow painted flowers nodding their heads
as if they were thoughtfully observing the clear afternoon
skies.

White birch trees waving their leaf-laden arms at
a chartreuse sweet gum they pretend to know
while the sweet gum stands stiffly ignoring them.

A white house dappled in a cloak of shadows,
silent and forlorn, as it waits for someone to iron
the wrinkles out of its peeling paint.

A pair of white bordered lawns, though not at all alike;
dancing alyssum rings the green one and
the brown one is caged by the white bones of dried shrubs.

A white painted sign on a curb nearby
reflects the sun like a shining star
blurring the numbers it holds.

A white cloud plays tag with the grasping green firs
who, each in turn, slap at its trailing legs
as it skips mockingly by.

A group of white daylilies bask in the sun
and argue about who has the best tans;
although none are qualified to judge.

FISHING

The green brown surface reveals nothing below
neither ripple nor shadow or reflection of light.
Are they there? They must be; where else would they go?
For all of their talents, they have no talent for flight.

They ignore my entreaties to sample the offering
I've placed before them to entice and delight.
I search the surface for signs of their going
and impatiently question, "When will they bite?"

Lifting the line to examine the bait;
do I expect it is gone, disappeared, out of sight?
No it is still there, unbitten, un-ate;
and I say to myself, "What a hell of a sight!"

In my mind I can hear them laughing and giggling
with shaking stomachs, mocking my plight
as the bait I've selected is writhing and wiggling.
They must bite soon for it is nearing the night.

A flick of the pole arcs the hook through the surface,
not where it was but two feet to the right.
Before, I am sure, it was hidden, lodged in a crevice.
Now that it's moved it's as free as a kite

to soar and dip and wave so inviting
that none can resist, try as they might.
The line twitches and jerks. Are they really biting?
Then I lean back and pull the line tight.

I strain at the pole; the line zigging and zagging
and pull this marine monster into the light.

As I throw the small perch back, I am thinking of bragging
about the huge bass that got away tonight.

AIR

How liquid and homogenous a medium it is
hanging motionless before us
caring not whether we see or feel its texture

Then slipping slowly away
carrying with it all that will join
dust, fog, seed, and spore

Or whipped into an angry tirade
bent on moving the very earth
to demonstrate its power

Lifting flora, fauna, rock, and water
To fling them down again
As punishment for their insolence

Air

How liquid and homogenous a medium it is
Yet given to every emotion

Invisible as the hand of God
But so obvious

I SAID

I meant what I said when I said it
I didn't mean it a moment before
I meant it not the next day and now
I can say that I cannot remember
the way it impressed me in that time
in the past when I said it at last after long
and deep thought whether should I or not
say something I meant on a subject so
small that I have forgotten completely what
affected me so deeply to compel me to
meekly say anything at all

CAROLE
DWINELL

TODAY, TOMORROW ... AND TOMORROW

Saying goodbye today,
Maybe it's hello tomorrow.
Or is this the twenty-four hours,
The pre-drawn divider folded down between
Pastdays with patented memories — and nextdays,
Blank pages filled with a turmoil of unthought?
I wait now in time's measured doorway,
With darkening hope of just one,
One last-ditch effort to stay
Cancer's black clock.

The effort of striving for
Unchange, rewind, a sequel,
A last-minute reprieve. Hold the familiar
Hands of the hall clock, ones that remember
When we ate dinner, made love, and drank wine.
The pendulum is hinting, it's time, it's time.
The day is a short one, ticks bring on the
Chimes, marching, timed to new hours ...
Oh, please stop that hand before
It executes the hour.

THE NIGHT LIST

The mind swims with thoughts of 'the list.'
Not the one written each evening to map my tomorrow.
Responsible content, in orderly fashion, the business
Of the day, the enterprise of the hours.

Minutes carefully planned, a personal catalog
Of calculated order, items and function
That when processed, accomplished, crossed off,
Will be a snapshot of life measured in time slots.

Archeologists of tomorrow will surely unearth
These rooms full of lists, the scribbles,
The chronicles of expectations, tasks that contain
Not a trace of heat, of camouflaged risk.

No elements of escape will remain recorded,
No document, inventory, account of flamboyant journeys.
No, a gallon of milk, pick up dry cleaning, P.T.A.,
A bit of this, too much of that, treading safe waters

All systematically recorded even as my mind ...
My mind swims recklessly, aimlessly
With thoughts of the 'unlist'
the 'unlist' of deeper more dangerous currents.

FENCE LINE

There is a fine line
between ecstasy and
terror, between air and
water, where the horses
should be and where
they should not...

Poetry is a fence line
between sanity and
chaos. Take words to the
fine line, the cliff,
both sides of the fence,
both sides of time.

Make sure you stay on
the horse.
Don't forget to shut the
gate ... or just maybe...

      you should

        ...open it.

WEEDS AND CHAOS

My garden is in disrepair
as it wakes up this spring,
with weeds and chaos everywhere
and I've not done a thing
to clear the ivy from the fence
or hide the other evidence
of slipshod gardening.

The lemon trees need care,
they have cobwebs in their hair,
and Rose of Sharon's weeping tears
of sorrow.

My ancient artichoke
seems just about to croak.
I guess I'd better intervene —

tomorrow.

ART LESSON

Parts of the picture
are plain to me —
the sky, the sun,
a house, a tree.
The artist's name is David,
with a backward "d."
Yes, David, grade 3.

Look, the sky is blue,
crayola blue,
with an orange sun
that casts no shadows.
Shadows don't come
until high school.

A plane hangs in the crayola sky
surrounded by puffs of flak.
See bombs falling from the plane
exploding on the ground
in plumes of crayola black.

At the side of the house
see the bodies on the lawn,
two women and a child?
The lawn is crayola green
and crimson.

THE GOLDEN OWL

"Make a poem like this," he said,
then showed me how to fit it together
like a golden owl,
vowels round and plump,
every feather sculpted,
and, in each amber eye, forever.

Intricate and precious too,
but the words were jiggered 'round
to fit some ancient pattern and
Ideas got fuzzed and fizzled out.

"That owl won't fly." I told him.
He smiled and said, "I know."

"If you take a baby's foot
natural and functional,
then break it, fold its toes under.
Mutilate it in the name of beauty.
You know damn well
such feet can't walk.
And this golden owl can't fly
because it is caged in a cruel format
in the name of beauty.

"Be god to your poem.
Focus on ideas instead of format.
Beauty happens when
feet walk and golden owls fly
free."

JOHN GOORY

UNTITLED

There once was a boy who had four friends
He would visit them regularly because each
Would usually tell him a story or give him a gift
When he would appear he would start in the
Direction and at the time of the rising of the sun.

Raphael in his garden at the rising of the sun
He wore yellow and was light and airy
And made me feel good with his smile
He gave me herbs he gave me a knife
To prepare them he gave me life

Michael in his woods was wondering
He wore red armor complete with helmet and sword
He felt as warm as the noon sun and as strong
He gave me a walking stick and a tinder box
To make fire and he gave me light

Gabriel walked by the ocean still and deep
His garment the same color as the water around him
He gave me a cup and a pouch filled with water
To carry on my journey and he gave me love

Auriel sat on a large stone with the darkness
Of midnight and the universe surrounding him.
In his green eyes truth and understanding shone
And I feared and was awed as I approached him
He gave me a book and a bookmarker
With a symbol on it   he gave me the law

WHAT TO DO ABOUT POWER STRUGGLES AT ALL LEVELS

Who has no power
has power
or so it seems
sometimes

Do not believe your own press
ask Paris Hilton or Lohan
about this

Better to be the power behind the throne
than the throne itself

Better to fight your battles within yourself
than not.

as above so below

The Gods need us as much as we need them

They need our belief in them
As much as we need their protection

Ask the Greek and Roman Gods about this

The original entity created the big bang
and the universe was born

But he/she/it was an artist and left to do other things
So the universe all creatures great and small
and of light and darkness
are evolving alone

The universe is a perfect whatever it is
and we are perfect within it.

So there is no need of outside help.
Do not believe your own press

THE AKASHIC RECORDS

If you stand before
the high priestess
and you pass her test
You may be shown the door
to what is generally called
the Akashic Records
These records contain
all the information
about the universe
in all dimensions
from the big bang
to the end of time
Various portions may be tapped
by anyone with authorization —
or by asking the head librarian
somewhere in the main library.
The information is given symbolically
must be interpreted by the user
may be used
however you want
The pathways and the
dimensions and the information
is finite in the sense
it is limited to our universe
and what is in it
It is the largest information
retrieval system there is
and all you need to get there
is to pass the firewall
established by your unconscious
fear and anxiously
apply for your library card now
and search the stacks yourself!

RONNA LEON

HARM'S WAY

The Great Blue Heron rises out of the marshy
wasteland at the foot of the oil refinery.
The bird, magnificent and unlikely blends
against the smoky sky like a misplaced puzzle piece.
I keep thinking how I'd never let a child
wade in those waters.
The Heron sees the refinery ponds as wetland.
He's like my son who's joined the army.
My son believes the army holds opportunity.
He doesn't fear the pond's hidden hazards.
They're both free creatures in harm's way.

DELETING EMILY

My husband subscribed to an on-line service
that sends Emily Dickinson's poems to me.
It's done at 2:30 a.m. each morning:
my computer records the exact hour of sending.

I see Emily in her white cotton night gown –
wide flat collar and embroidered cuffs.
She crouches down to open the wicker box
she keeps under her narrow bed.
Her important father sleeps down the hall.
She does not light her candle for fear of disturbing.
The box holds the fair copies of her poems,
those poems they'll finally read after she is dead.
Her delicate hands search the stack
selecting the perfect one to send.

continued next page

RONNA LEON

continued from previous page

Even when I don't sleep well, her poem
is there when I open my mailbox.
I'm on 242, an epitaph, of four hundred and forty four.
Emily greets me each morning - her quick, stubborn mind,
her girlish flirtation with men and nature.
She often makes me laugh,
an old maid, that Emily, with a few fine secrets.
She has a nervous refinement, and a querying conscience.

For months I collected each of Emily's efforts,
printed some to post on the refrigerator, read others into
the record.
I couldn't bring myself to delete a single one, even knowing
I had a book of her complete works left over from college days.
If I could've tied the computer poems in a satin ribbon,
I would have done so like letters from my sweetest friend.

It happened inadvertently, I swear it;
fits of housekeeping bring such woes.
I deleted Emily, I saw her go, a sound I won't forget,
a whoosh and she was gone, returned perhaps to Amherst,
perhaps to some literary file,
or maybe to that heaven she questioned would prove real.
Relief only in remembering she'll return tomorrow,
she doesn't hold a grudge, she'll send a poem again
spare and cool at dawn - number two hundred and forty
three.

CONUNDRUM

Maybe it isn't one thing
but another.
Maybe the time isn't right.
The baby's been thrown out
with the bath water.
The black hole sucked up the light.

Caution tape's always bright yellow.
Chalk marks where the bodies lie.
The front door is triple locked.
The supermarket's open all night.

Maybe truth IS stranger than fiction.
Maybe the postman rings twice.

If I had to place bets,
if I want to win big,
if facts can be trusted,
if I've got this right,
further research proves necessary
more often than not.

JUANITA J. MARTIN

PORTRAIT: THE ASHES ARE STILL BURNING

My bed, empty as my desolate heart,
leaves me at the edge, holding onto the past.
Sunlight peeks into my window,
as another day rudely awakens me.

I lie here staring. Two-toned blues pour out their sadness;
how the walls match my soul!
Remembering makes time stand still,
while visions of love hurt me so.

Eyes release nocturnal clouds,
while feelings of misery lie inside.
I am a silent wanderer in the dark, hiding from shadows.
Instrusive sounds now fill my ears,
exchanging passion for a cup of starting fluid.

ONE MAN'S TREASURE

He rises like a soldier, a diligent hero
before the dawn, dressed for battle.
Hydraulics wail like sirens,
as arms of steel crush maggot-filled waste.
His hands are exposed to life's dirty side.
They tell the tales of the mundane, the innocent,
the forbidden trails we blaze.
He disposes of the unwanted, the broken, the old.
Beyond the repulsive piles, are rare finds,
pieces of history, the only rewards this humble servant
rarely receives. He's a relic too.
He's stood the test of time, economic despair.
He disappears like a ghost, dismissed, until pyramids
of decay plague the masses.
Amidst the vile rubbish, he emerges,
the scent of an unlikely saviour.

REFLECTIONS OF SUMMER

Accents of flowers sprinkle the earth,
as burgeoning colors perpetuate their beauty.
Soft clouds line a pale blue sky,
while cool water caresses a mountainside.

Warm breezes sashay a grassy terrain,
upstaged by smoky pits in the distance,
as vacationers seek solace
in the season's pagentry.

Temperatures rise to unbearable heights,
while dusty lanes lead closer to home.
Walking alone multiplies the hours,
as sweat beads upon my face.

Sounds of water fascinate,
as the lake comes into view.
Bathers bask in the glow of a steamy sun,
not bothered by an envious stare.

Iron-pumped torsos in skimpy apparel
swarm cabins nearby.
Just beyond the hills, an inner city awakens.
Billboards flicker, as ardous days become fun-filled nights.

BOXCAR ANGEL

Steel cages with no bars became
    a refuge to the disheveled man.
He gazed down the tracks,
    conjuring evil thoughts about his past,
as he peered into its window.
He saw the cold, he felt the cold,
    seeping into his bones.
It blew in like a ghost, rattling its chains.
Nightfall closed in, took away his light,
    which also warmed him.

As ice formed outside, the weary man
    lay frostbitten on his own metal grave.
The inevitale doom was taking place,
    when the door opened.
Everything disappeared
    into a mysterious cloud,
as the iron horse roared to a halt.
    Dawn tapped the man awake,
relinquishing the previous ordeal.

His languid lips formed a smile,
    as the sun shone brightly.
This man felt lifted to a place of hope,
    with a new order for his feet;

    this was not his last stop.

MICHAEL
MERRIS

HAWK AT 7 A.M.
for Rachel B.

Dorothea Lange's light frames
hawk fiercer than fear
flowing from night tangle hair
thru Tor tower.
magnificent
magnanimous.
meaning
scoured
in Phoenix rising
from despair's seduction.
this whispers God
life
intimacy:
thank you.

A MOTHER'S DAY POEM
to Liza Dodd

I p.s.'d your
Mother's Day card
"thank you for supporting my writing."
you said in response,
"I don't know..I am not a poet…"
I interrupted,
"You once said that I shine when I write.
No one had said that before or since."
after that we
ate our sandwiches
and watched the boys play
as puppies
on grass.
I drifted the
afternoon
in easiness of
togetherness
and got what I
always wanted with you
peace:
and you know what,
it was marvelous.
20 years and
and our scared family's hearts;
I ponder my part in the price.
I ponder my part in the peace.

THE WAY A WOMAN'S EYES SMILE

to Sue D.

you can see when a woman
has a new man in her life
in her eyes.
her laugh lilts
and her smile,
well, it spells Barbie, doll houses that were packed away
too long ago, ballerina slippers,
the prince with a horse
that doesn't need to be house broken
and holding his shaking freckled hand
until he can't remember her name,
satisfaction
and the awe of hope.
not the memory of the last
son of bitch
that she threw out.
kid,
let me quit
this parlor game
and get down to
it.
we are all pulling for you
to be happy
to have joy
to find someone who won't run
no matter what
and be loyal
to your last breath.
for your struggle gives
 us hope

DEBRALEE PAGAN

URBAN HERMIT

Single at sixty
Sanguine, but O, so alone!,
we think. She overhears. Says,
use your eyes, friends, use your ears!

The grit that sits in parking lots,
the fungus slowly seeping into speed bumps,
They witness me.

The coke-can sculptures
in low vacant lots,
the weeds with crinkled heads
which mediate the glory of sundown;
the slanted light hung down
unraveling plaster,
They cherish me.

The dying sapling on the corner
with its leaves that droop and dart like schools of fishes,
dancing
whirlpools into autumn windshields,
They applaud me.

The rusty stairway to the fire escape
where no one ever stands,
the undeveloped alley with
its walls of brick on either hand;
We mutely fray down to decay
that will not renovate.
We'll be torn down. But
They accompany me
into loud anonymity.
Not once —
Never Once In My Life —
Have I been alone.

DEBRALEE PAGAN

THE NEW GUY

My mind is like a tumble dryer
thrashing and spinning the same two garments
over and over in one round window:
Sunday's date. Tuesday's date.
The grey part is his eyes.
The pink part is my hope.

I have better things to do,
but I sit and watch the dryer
and I yearn, I lean -
his chest beneath my cheek,
hard and lean
- and speculate on my chances
any?
many?
also lean?
...knowing very well
that two small garments
are not enough for a load.

MESSAGES
for Jimmy Hurd, died 4/21/06

They met like prisoners
in closed up cubicles
from East and West
divided by a pane of glass,
steel reinforced,
no opening between.

They tried to trace
the pads of fingers –
pink with pulse and white with pressure –
moving mouths, and thought they heard
perhaps a low vibration

but after this
each went away
unsatisfied?
replete?

What can be read
from blurs and smears
and panted condensation?
Some Thing,
both strained and desperate
was exchanged here.
O, but what?

I made the marks.
I cannot give the answer.

DEBRALEE PAGAN

DON PEERY

ROSE HILL CEMETERY
Black Diamond Mines, California

Laura

Did you just stumble on my last sandstone brick?
That one is all that still remains of those that John
set here to mark our resting place. He brought one
or two each week, dug by his own strong hands
out of the sandstone core of the cold, dark underground.
He wanted me to be his wife, but my Pa would not
approve. Pa knew a miner's life was hard and said
that I should save myself, move on and find another.
If not for John, I might have gone, although I really
don't know where. Most women's lot is to have kids
and raise them for their man. And anywhere I might
have gone, my task would have been the same – besides
I liked John and he loved me (he told me so,
so many times). With Mother gone, I had Pa's
son and my two sisters yet to raise, so I
told John that we would have to wait. That winter, when
the fever came, my brother and youngest sister took ill.
Pa had to work the mine, so I tended them
day and night. It was harsh with so much else
to do, but I knew it would kill my Pa
to lose his only son so I did what I had
to do. It was hard, but he and my sister survived.
I was so tired – that must by why I caught it then
and why it took me so fast. I had no strength left
to fight it off and spent my last breath calling
John. My Pa had nothing much to pay a proper
preacher, so John and him dug my grave and built
the box to put me in and laid me here among
the rest. Each Sunday afternoon, John would come
to sit and talk about the week just past. And he
would bring a stone from the mine, dug and shaped

by his own hand to mark a square for me and,
he said, for him. It was hard to tell, but when
he left me there each Sunday, his step seemed lighter, his heart
less heavy. Through spring, summer and early fall he came
until, in late November, he brought the double stone
to set up in our square. On my side he had carved
my name, date of birth and date of death. The other
side he carved his own name – reserved, he said, for later.
That winter it snowed a bit, but every Sunday he
was there and I would stir against his presence and bade
the wind to speak his name. And then one Sunday nearing
spring, he came a final time. They bore him up
beneath a bright warming sun and sky of frosted
blue and laid him down at my left hand. And so
in death, we have lain together here as we
had not in life for near a hundred-twenty years.

John

Laura lies at my right hand – I insisted
that it be that way. So when the mine caved in
and laid me out, they brought me here and put me down.
In truth, my heart was here already – my love possessed
of her. And though my body walked and worked and prayed,
my mind was full of Laura's soul. Her father was
a miner too and wanted better for his girl,
but there weren't many better here than us that worked
the veins of coal. Five towns grew up within an hour's
walk to house our folk, a company store and workmen's
bars but not much else, for few would come so far
away from better places. And so we'd meet on Sundays,
she young and fair and me not too much her elder
so that I could hope that she would someday be
my wife. It was winter when the fever came
and medicines were scarce. She burned her life away

— *continued next page*

DON PEERY   51

— *continued from previous page page*

saving her brother and youngest sister. The last words
upon her lips, her father said, had been my name.
All were poor here abouts and I had little
to help her father out. I cut her name into
a board and set it at her head to mark her grave.
Each Sunday I would come bearing a sandstone brick
from the mine that I had cut and shaped to place
upon the ground to mark what would be our square.
Then I would sit and speak awhile and share the news
as I had heard of all that happened in our towns…
a poor replacement for her life but all I had
to offer her. Yet slowly I saved enough 'til
finally I could buy a stone to proper mark
her resting place. I brought it here and set it up
myself and finished marking out our square. I must
have known what time I had – or else had held it off
so I could consecrate our space before the tunnel
ceiling fell. And so we rest together now in death
as we had not in life. Yet I am content,
Laura lying at my right hand side, awaiting
love's renewal bright in God's redeeming light.

DON PEERY

JEANNE
POWELL

SWING DANCE
for my mother

When you left me to go hide
in that silk-lined casket
I pulled fresh dandelions
and hid them in my coat
until the grave diggers
rested their shovels.
I scattered your lioness dandies
on the dirt covering your new home.
Near the end of my childish days
you always did travel without me.
This cemetery trick was no new game.

To see you dance once more
to that swing music you liked on the radio
when you thought no one was watching
recalling a time before husband
and kids and worries
when you worked swing shift
with all the other Rosies
then danced the night away.
To hear you laugh once more
would have been sweet.

WHEN I WAS

When
I was
just a girl
parents
invariably commanded
me to be
quiet,
more "still,"
free of freedom
because
childhood requires
training, sacrifice, breaking.
Notice
news is
breaking news today.
Have
you witnessed
this phenomenal, mad
phrasing?
People believing,
as they must,
that
broken is
the perfect way.

REFLECTING

Let me start over
I like everything about him

the way he hurls impatience at men friends
down on their luck who hide out
too long on his living room floor

he caresses a surpentine cat
who guards the steep winding staircase
to his private world

he laughs about the train wrecks
littering his love life

he makes minestrone from scratch
the way his grandmother taught

he stretches nice and slow
filling the doorway without a sound

he caresses a guitar before rippling its strings
into soundblasts of anger

he waits free of time and judgment
for the old scars of a new friend to heal

he is a nurturing silence
with saki at sunset

let me start over
I like everything about him

JOHN
ROBERT
PRAY

TREE

Seven times,
the old oak let go
a limb, keeping only the scars
to circle barkless up its trunk.

Seven times,
disrepecting nesting quail,
we cut each limb to firewood.

Seven winters,
we burned the firewood,
log after glorious log.

Dangerous work —
two valleys over
a man was killed cutting wood;
and, my neighbor lost his foot,
well, half his foot.
Limbs can jump up and turn on you,
something to do with gravity.

The good news is,
if you don't get killed or crippled,
it is manly fun,
and you get to keep warm all winter.

All those scars:
it lives because of sacrifice,
seven times seven times seven —
the feeling of a sacred number.
I walk around it, looking up.
All those scars,
but it never stops growing.

JOHN ROBERT PRAY

BENICIA

This is not the world.
This town is without that
inflatable facade,
the monotonous machinery
pumping images of spin and spit.

This place is without panic,
and there is escape
here for life to happen
in step with the seasons.
The wind can be felt.
A quiet river can be sensed,
a part of history flowing.

People, self-cultivating,
exchange survival recipes,
volumes of the best,
good advice for travelers
about to go into the world.

THAT FOOL

That fool wanted a hat.
He imagined one
on the top of his head,
fitting him perfectly.

Walking in the rain,
wearing his imaginary hat,
he got wet.
He caught cold.

Afraid of dying,
that fool wanted a halo.

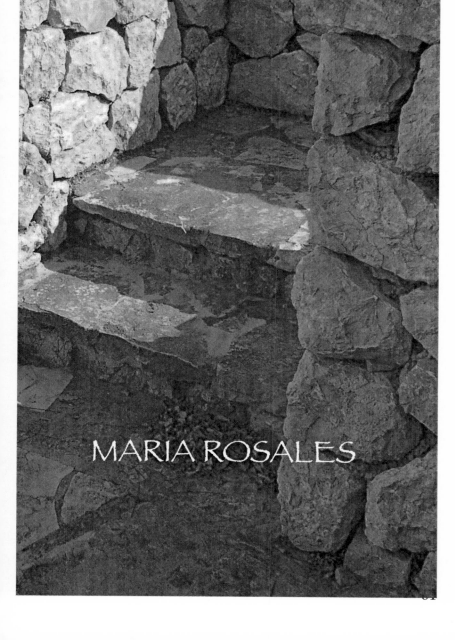

MARIA ROSALES

IF THIS WERE MY LAST DAY

If this were my last day
I would let the cat sit on my lap right now, as I type.
If this were my last day
I would forego sleep to write this poem.

I would step outside this morning without shoes,
to watch the sun rise over Mount Diablo.
I would walk the dog before taking my coffee,
spend an extra languid hour by the lake.

If this were my last day
I would wear something frivolous to the garden,
loll in the hammock in satin or silk,
reciting my poems to the birds, or to the pastel dawn.

If this were my last day
I would reel all my grudges in like fish,
take the hooks out, and let them free,
so I could call those who hurt me and love them anyway.

I would surprise myself with tenderness for my enemies,
sip jasmine tea and eat dessert twice,
look in the eyes of everyone I meet,
let them know, out loud, or in silence,

that they matter, and are loved.
I would be an ambassador of peace in my world.

If this were my last day
I would play before my bed was made, and make a happy
mess
in the kitchen, baking complicated cookies from scratch,
naked except for a starched apron.

If this were my last day, looking back or forward
would make no difference. And I would be at peace with that.

If this were my last day, my children would know
that I am ready, and they would release me with joy.
I would not slip softly into the dark river,
but shoot like a rainbow-tailed comet into oblivion.

SLEEPWALKER

I am putting one foot in front of the other.
My world is tilting,
my eyes not quite focused, gait unsteady.
Excuse me if I stutter or bump into you.

Do you feel the world tilting
under all this hatred and blood?
Excuse me if I stutter or bump into you,
I am doing the best I can.

Written before all this hatred and blood,
prophesies I don't believe
(though I do the best I can)
seem, anyhow, to be coming true.

Prophesies? I don't believe
fate has us in a chokehold,
yet my nightmares seem to be coming true.
The alarm is sounding while I sleep.

Fate has me in a chokehold.
My eyes unfocused, gait unsteady,
with all alarms sounding, I walk asleep,
putting one foot in front of the other.

DESERT ECHOES

This desert room holds little of me –
Most objects speak of your history, not mine.
Do I have a history, now that you took my name?

I search for objects that remained through many lives and loves.
There are only two – my totems.
My father's mandolin,
and the beads from an afghan wedding dress.

The mandolin wails only in memory,
the curve of its belly is its own pregnant coffin.
My father's silken tenor locked now in other wood.

The dress found me as I sailed
past an Afghan merchant's trendy barrow
Portobello Road, 1976.
Patched with velvet, laden with hopeful beads.

I wore it while my son swam in my belly. Dreamed
of caravans,
     bearing figs,
          following stars.

I took it to the tropics.
Its hand-woven heaviness doomed it to exile
in a musty humid closet. It died. The beads remain.
Some farmer's daughter a hundred years ago

kept her dowry to her chest, folded in the beaded pockets.
The dress billowed behind her in the vermillion desert wind.
She haunted my pregnancy, wailed for her dowry's return,

an Afghan banshee. These many years, I still hear her keening
in the back doors of my mind, in the quiet places I nurture
outside of our story. This desert room holds little of me –

I create a vessel in my soul,
     fill it with myself.

SHERRY
SHEEHAN

CARQUINEZ FROG

Like a frog
on a smooth stone
near a pond,

I lie all morning
under the leafy sheets
of my bed

not moving,
only breathing
while waiting

for a flyspeck
of desire
to prod me into action.

My pond, the Carquinez Strait,
lies at least a mile from here,
more than an hour's hopping,

but I remember a closer pond,
empty in the next room,
the clawfoot tub.

I'll start the water in it,
rub the mud from my thinking,
and soak until I'm human.

SHERRY SHEEHAN

KO'OLAU

I tip my head back to my spine
to see the tops of Ko'olau's cliffs,
O'ahu's 3,000-foot-high eastern lip.
Its base is nearly close enough to touch.
Like a Waikiki high rise, it goes straight up,
replacing sky with mossy stone.

This afternoon it tickles clouds on their race
over the Pacific and launches a hang glider
who swoops down to hover over me.
Wrapped to his chest in a windsock,
he swivels and circles – a giant dragonfly,
slowly descending. Drifting closer,
he kicks apart his body's canvas
to let his legs dangle before landing,

detaching his wings, and walking toward me.
I, a smaller bug, wingless and long trapped
by gravity, welcome the sky whiffs
and cliff moss he brings me, both of us
grinning at our spectacular insignificance.

MORGUE.ORG

after 1973's movie "Soylent Green"

If morgue.org is a place
you can find in Web space,
then calm.com must be
clickable too.

I'd go to the latter
to plan for the former
after worse
than a lingering flu.

I'd get myself pills,
shipped fast and tax free,
and like Edward G.,
I'd follow the drill,
lying back to enjoy
earth's best scenery,

then pop what I'd got
and let "Soylent Green"
in its advertised scheme
send me off in a dream.

It's one way to go
and better than some.
When 'whatever' goes bad,
when joints are not plumb,
when too much stays sad
in the middle of fun,
when you've lost all you had,
time to join Dad & Mum.

'

ROBERT
M. SHELBY

ROW TO THE RAINBOW AND SET SAIL

A patchwork morning streams;
a flown-down bluebird folds his wings
as notes from his white throat throb widely loud
with clear, rebounding screams
of sea-gulls wheeling as he sings
under their windy *pas-de-pluie* of cloud.

Will this bird heed the misty beams
of sunlight firing up the noisy beach
to our dim-eyed appreciation? Are we proud
to be above the wavelets, each on each
advancing and retiring with cross institution
confused and practicing a mutual infusion?

We should advance with day.
We should enjoy the short row out
to your new yacht so jauntily riding
the quick-swell ruffled bay.
We should allow no shoreward doubt
to keep us on the pier, busily hiding
from wet getting underweigh
Your "Rainbow Castle" is a likely craft
unreefed, and with an orthodox and low-abiding
will to right itself as any raft,
so you should set a plaque above her galley door:
"This peaceful minds float justly
                            on their endless war."

ROBERT M. SHELBY

HARD ELOQUENCE

The dead sculptors are silent. The living
attend their own dreams. Techniques. New media.
News. They ignore the ancestor.
      As when seldom they work in stone,
machine tools in hand, they hear carbide
intone songs tangently around sought form.
They no longer hear stone.
      Stone, are you granite or marble
to be cut and ground, pounded, fretted and polished?
Do you keep silent at fracture
when you are split off from yourself,
separated from your like into another likeness?
      Tell us how it is, to be chiseled off
and discarded from a statue, or worse
from an abstract piece with a cute name,
a figure for nothing in particular.

BALLADE ON A SLY ASSASSIN

Paris, late fall night, reign of Louis XIII

Streets are dark and we are armed
but, as you see, my blade is quiet.
Mutual friends would be quite charmed
to see you struggle and defy it ...
I want peace and don't deny it.
No! — their guiles have not deceived me;
then sell unction. We won't buy it.
This one thing my father bequeathed me ...

Oh, I say, don't be alarmed!
Since his death in last year's riot
I am bound it not be harmed.
See this scabbard? Please, don't try it,
hardy use will only wry it.
Such fine workmanship! It grieved me,
that bloodstone, I had to pry it.
This one thing my father bequeathed me,

Yet that stone had to be farmed
else I had been on slender diet.
Better times, well dined and marmed,
I hastened right back to rebuy it.
Still, the jeweller did not guy it
Well, or scorn had not recieved me
sweetly as before ... Ah, fie it,
this one thing my father bequeathed me.

Closer. Under the flame here. Eye it?
Glad I am, you trust and believed me
while I draw now and apply *it*
this other thing my father bequeathed me!

ELAINE STARKMAN

GUALALA, 1985

This cove of water contains
what beaches in my mind:

my grandmother's death
nine months before my birth
floats to the surface
to tell me I'm now three years
past her final age

Flocks of gulls leaning into wind
a lone figure leaning into light
against the rocks
Each yields to nature in its own time
The wilderness of ocean rests momentarily

Our new dog that replaces
the old dead one lunges in the water
and in and out of the shoreline
with a joy that infuses our own
love that thinks itself omnipotent

Fog that obliterates first seals
then kelp

then me
    then you

ELAINE STARKMAN

CABANA CARIOCA, NEW YORK CITY
for Florence Miller

Only five hours and forty minutes
to New York air thick with excitement
of girlish adolescence in love
with new kid on the block.
She greets me and I become
the woman I want to be
in a city of strangers;
throw off the surf board I've never owned.
California landscapes collapse,
and here I swim into tough
streams of the street.
She floats me along.
We abandon ourselves
to every dark face and pan-handler
selling Swiss, Rolex, and Movados ...
We swoon at stocky waiters
in Cabana Carioca on 45th Street,
so Latin they still hate English.
Through her eyes I love these faces
as we samba up the line in step
to the last Portuguese buffet
where we pay just the counter price
for paella and flan at this lunch of love.

NIGHT EATER

I've eaten the chocolate in the bowl
searched the drawers through the night

Kisses, crackers, and caramel bites
I won't dare devour in daylight

What I yearn for, I do not know
to end this weakness, once and for all

or bleed it slowly
Thus imagine love unseen

not among butter and cream
but fall back on a stronger self:

When my taste is in need
it's my soul, not my mouth

CALIFORNIA COYOTE

Is he a mangy dog? Does he depend on neighbors leaving
out food, trying to tame him?
His yip and yowl have stopped dead. He too has stopped:
dog-tired confused tail down in the midst of suburban
streets. Twice I've seen him. He isn't bold or clever. Dead
eyed, sickly scapegoat, no illegal immigrant, no purposeful
trickster but lost animal soul that, like us, can't find
purpose or place in this maze of planned housing.

MARYANNE LESLIE
VILLARAZA-
SAULSBURY

MY ALCATRAZ

There you are again
Sitting alone right
Smack in the middle
Of this vast body of life…
What ails you
That you've become a castaway---
Those walls so locked you up;
You've become your own prisoner…
No escape from the world's angst and anger.
Justify what caused your crime;
Tell me why you sit there
Lonely, untouched and unloved!
As you write on
Your journal your secrets and lies
Who knows the truth but you?
Can you pass life
Unenlightened and not free to love;
How can you be paroled
From the sentence that was self-imposed?
Dare walk away from passion,
Pulling your heart back
Retreating to time when
You did not know me
When you did not love me.
You've always been an island
Seems like you prefer that.
Will you ever let me in again
My Rock, My Alcatraz
To free you from a life
Unyielding, unsatisfying?

A MAKESHIFT BED

A year ago I was in the same place…
Once again, I find myself
On a lowly mattress on the floor.
Alone and afraid.
This is that same feeling.
A familiar feeling of grief …
A loss so big that nothing around me
Can provide any bit of comfort or relief.
The pain is inside me … so deep.
I feel the need to grasp for some air;
I need to swim to the surface
As I can no longer hold my breath under water.
I am unable to see light …
This darkness is wrapped
All inside me; outside of me.
If there is one thing I feel okay doing,
It is to cuddle these eight pillows
On my humble makeshift bed.
I try to find a comfy spot.
The strain on my back and ulcer attack is bad.
I know it will take another dose of melatonin
                              to put me to sleep.
For now, I am allowing myself to cry …
To embrace these emotions …

CONCERT

1-13-09 / 5:10pm

Waves splash on deck
Lonely seagull squawks
Watching riders
Read paperbacks
Typing on keys
Scrolling the web
With tiny gadgets
Ears plugged as iTunes blare
And lost strangers dance
As ferry touches land.

Pavement welcomes
Heels and boots
Streetcars load
Suits and hats
As elevators and escalators
Ascend, descend.
Sliding doors need no doorman
They rush in single file.

Clockwatchers take notes
At board meetings
Shaking hands
Closing deals
Earning their keep
Taking coffee and cigarette breaks…

At half past five
Cars pile on bridges
Paying tolls
Weaving in and out
Of lanes
As carpool passes traffic jams.

Trains and buses
Carry loads of hungry folks
Missing sunset off horizon
Packed like sardines
On lookout
For vacant seats.

Waves splash on deck
Lonely rider watches
Seagull taunts blackbird
As ferry touches land
Driver gets home to end
A long day of symphony.

MARYANNE LESLIE VILLARAZA-SAULSBURY

THE POETS

Tamra Jane Amato

Tamra Jane Amato has lived in California since 1963, when she moved to the San Francisco Bay Area from South Dakota. A resident of Benicia since 1986, she graduated from UC Sonoma in 1975 and loves Art, all the Arts and a good joke.

Francis Anderson-Jackson

Having come late to poetry, it is no small thing for me to be included in these pages, proving once again that it is seldom *too* late. What do I want you to know about me? I am a woman. I'm like you and unlike you; smart and foolish; carelessly cruel but kinder now.; and puzzled by certain aspects of human behavior and questions of faith. This selection reflect my struggle for answers and reluctance to accept what the answer may have to be. While these poems began as an experiential journal for myself, they will journey on. How surprisingly sweet to hold this book in my hand ... and then give it away.

Peter Bray

Peter Bray is a graduate design engineer from UC Berkeley. He became an illustrator, graphic designer, supervisor and manager. He then fell off the corporate horse, learned how to clean sewer lines, fix sinks, sagging gates and wrote poetry and songs along the way. He writes a column for the Benicia Herald each Friday, *The A Capella Handyman* and longs to be either Rich and Famous or Pesky and Notorious. The latter two seem to be working. Check him out at www.peterbray.org. His songs are also on YouTube and FaceBook.

Suzanne Bruce

Suzanne Bruce, born and raised in Oklahoma, holds a B.S. in Education from the University of Tulsa. She did graduate work at Wichita State University in Childhood Behavior Disorders. She cherishes relaxing moments by the ocean, finding it meditational and inspirational. She continues her poetry writing singularly, as well as doing collaborative (ekphrastic) work with artist Janet Manalo. Their book is *Voices Beyond the Canvas* (2007). http://www.ekphrasticexpressions.com

Chuck Conner

Writing poetry is a relatively recent career move for Chuck. Having completed careers in the military and civilian telecommunications he is delighted to be pursuing a more personal interest. Chuck has always held learning as a most important pursuit and he has learned by experience. From soda jerk to nuclear power operator, from Coast Guard Officer to cotton picker, every learning experience has added to the color and variety of his poetry.

Carole Dwinell

Writing forever, Carole has had her work appear in the First Tuesday Anthology series which she helped produce, as well as — *Finding What You Didn't Lose* by John Fox / publisher Tarcher Putnam, *DrumVoices Review, Berkeley, City of Buds and Flowers,* and a chapbook of her own, *Looking Sideways.* She works as a freelance photojournalist for both trade and web magazines. Dwinell is a fine artist, and lives on a small horse ranch near Martinez, California. See: www.caroledwinell.com

Joel Fallon

A San Francisco native, Joel now, [and deservedly so — *ed.*] is Benicia's first Poet Laureate Emeritus. His captivating, serious and occasionally tongue-in-cheek work has been heard and enjoyed throughout the San Francisco Bay Area.

John Goory

John Goory reaches into his mind, into the universe and his handmade and decorated tarot cards to divine the unexplainable, to define one's needs and desires. From Chicago to Los Angeles to Benicia via Mill Valley and Santa Rosa, he is searching for the techno-pagan well-versed in PhotoShop while serving as the Director of Cinnabar — the Crystalline Center of Infinite Possibilities. He hopes for a publisher of his Tarot deck.

Ronna Leon

Poems are like whispered secrets and the poet is the heart of it. True stories and the best gossip reside in the poet's work, not bios and résumés. Ronna Leon has lived in Benicia for a long long time. She takes on the city's adventures in words and language as the Benicia Poet Laureate for 2010-2012.

Juanita J. Martin

Juanita J. Martin is a multi-talented, award-winning poet. Her poetry appears in *Blue Collar Review*, *Soma Literary Review* and *Rattlesnake Review*. A freelance writer and performance artist, she's a member of the Ina Coolbrith Circle, Poetry Society of America, & California Writers Club-Redwood Branch.

Michael Merris

M.R. Merris was born Feb. 12, 1953. in Jacksonville Illinois. Started writing poetry in the 8th grade as a class assignment where his first attempt earned an F. Started drinking at 13 and was a black out drinker by age 15. Shipped as merchant seaman for two years and then enlisted in USN. In the '80s, clean and sober, he returned to civilian life and has lived in the S.F. Bay Area ever since. Married late and was divorced after 15 years. Has two sons. Six months after he left the marriage he was laid off from his job of 15 years. He has been employed for two years out of the last six. Homeless in Nov. 2008. Heart attack three months later on his 56th birthday. Currently working on book of stories titled *Waving Goodbye*. Trying to find a publisher for his second book of poems, *Smoked Topaz*.

Debralee Pagan

Debralee Pagan is the poetry pen name of Deborah Fruchey, who got tired of having her name mispronounced. Deborah has appeared in six anthologies and numerous literary journals, and publishes a free monthly poetry newsletter, *Strictly East*. You can visit her at www.lafruche. net. Her new self-help manual, *Is There Room for Me, Too? 12 Steps and 12 Strategies for Coping with Mental Illness*, will be available shortly on Amazon.com.

Don Peery

Taking a trip through Don Peery's *Coffee House Reflections*, the journey sips and stirs up memories of road trips, of observation ... and somehow of love and loss. Within the venue of a plethora of coffee bean bistros, the poetry and the photos speak of and perhaps for us all.

Jeanne Powell

Jeanne Powell is a poet and fiction writer. Several of her poems have won awards. She is the author of *My Own Silence* (2006) and *Word Dancing* (2008). For more than ten years she has hosted spoken word events in San Francisco. Visit http://www.redroom.com/author/jeanne-powell

John Robert Pray

Having been published in several anthologies, hosted the open mike at Peet's Coffee in Fairfield, and judged poetry competitions, John Robert Pray is convinced that much evolves from our poetry. He says that writing poetry is like exercising another pair of hands.

Maria Rosales

Maria Rosales was born in London, and lived abroad and in Hawaii before settling in California. Her poems have appeared in *Byline, Poetry Depth Quarterly, Poetalk, Meridian,* and *The Nashville Newsletter,* and several anthologies as well as the Online magazine *Dirty Napkin.* See http://www.dirtynapkin.com. She has won numerous awards from the Ina Coolbrith Circle and Artists Embassy International. Maria hosted the PrimoPoets series in the East Bay for several years. She and her husband, Marco, are building a retreat for Artists in Yucatan, Mexico. Currently, Maria serves as a contributing editor for the online magazine *ARTBEAT,* published by the Arts and Culture Commission of Contra Costa County.

Sherry Sheehan

Born and brought up in Hawaii, Sherry was a school psychologist in Las Vegas before retiring to Crockett. Since 2006 she has been poet laureate for Ed Dewke's psoriasis web site http://www.flakehq. com and has also enjoyed writing poems for paintings by Robert Chapla (see their *Across Currents*), Mary Reusch (*PoArtry*), and other artists (see http://sites.google.com/site/sherrysheehanpoems/ and http://poetrymatters.150m.com) as well as participating in ekphrastic exhibits with Mary Reusch in Michigan and Indiana; with Suzanne Bruce, Janet Manalo, and Robert Chapla in Fairfield; and in Danville, Livermore and Martinez ekphrastic events.

Robert Shelby

Robert M. Shelby is the second Benicia Poet Laureate, serving from 2008 until 2010. He has listened to poetry and crafted his poems from a very young age to the encouragement and exposure to "vibrantly crafted language" given by his parents. He said in the very first *Every First Tuesday,* that only poetry "... has engaged me, both for its growing results and evocation of that intangible which, in fact, not myth, extends us ..." His careful attention to the form and history of the written poem reveals itself as one reads his work. He has published several chapbooks and has been instrumental in encouraging others to do the same.

Elaine Starkman

Mixed in with her love of learning, her love of Judaism, nature, and being a published author, Elaine Starkman is a poet as her work in this anthology will attest. But she is more. She has recently co-authored *"My Dreaming Waking Life: Six Poets, 66 Poems*, found on Amazon.com. She is the author of *Learning to Sit in the Silence: Journal of Caretaking* and the co-editor of *Here I Am: Contemporary Jewish Stories from Around the World*, which won the PEN/Oakland Award in 1999. Awards include winning the Benicia Love Contest (1995), and an award from the Ashville Writers School on a story about Beethoven. Contact is: Elaine.Starkman@gmail.com.

Maryanne Leslie Villaraza-Saulsbury

This is my journey. At twelve, I stumbled upon a poem entitled "Dust." Intrigued that words about dust could move me, I attempted to write poetry. I wrote for no one but myself; no intended reader, no intent to be edited nor published. I was safe and I hid behind the name "Dustles." At 23, I crossed the Pacific and landed in the Bay Area. I earned a new name and played different roles. I learned that I can be whatever I want to be. I have arrived but still did not want an audience. Sixteen years later, I was given a second lease on life. A near death experience shook my core … my being. I found my voice, my heart, my soul. So here I am. This is me … living my life of right and wrong, love and hate, smiles and tears, courage and fear and of life and death.

INDEX OF POEMS

Colphon
Windows and Skylights

Cover is printed in four color process on 90# Ultra Smooth Cover, white
Interior pages printed in black on 55# Colonial White Creme
Both are ANSI standard for archival quality paper

Typography:
Cover and Poets' Names are in Papyrus
Poems, Indices, Bios in Palatino

Photography:
Cover and pages 1, 5, 17, 21, 29, 41[1], 45, 53, 57, 65, 69, 73, 82 (of Amato),
83 (of Dwinell), 84 (for Martin), 85 (of Merris), 85 (for Peery), 86 (for
Powell), 88 (of Villaraza-Saulsbury) — *Carole Dwinell*

Pages 33, 82 (of Bray), 83 (of Conner), 84 (of Leon), 85 (of Pagan), 86 (of
Pray and Rosales) — *Ronna Leon*

Photos courtesy of the poets:
Page 9 Peter Bray, 13 and 83 Suzanne Bruce, 25 Joel Fallon,
37 Juanita Martin, 45 Robert Hamaker, 49 Don Peery, 61 Maria Rosales,
77 Maryanne Leslie Villaraza Saulsbury, 82 Francis Anderson-Jackson,
86 Sherry Sheehan, 87 Robert Shelby, 88 Elaine Starkman.

[1] *photo was taken of an injured non-releasable red-tailed hawk at Lindsay Wildlife
Museum, Walnut Creek, California. Used with the permission of the Museum and US
Game and Wildlife.*

Breinigsville, PA USA
01 December 2010
250410BV00001B/1/P

WINDOWS & SKYLIGHTS

Anthology Number Three

Benicia First Tuesday Poets

Outskirts Press, Inc.
Denver, Colorado

Windows & Skylights
Anthology Number Three
All Rights Reserved.
Copyright © 2010 Benicia First Tuesday Poets

V3.0

Outskirts Press, Inc.
http://www.outskirtspress.com

ISBN: 978-1-4327-6343-5

Library of Congress Control Number: 2010936271

Outskirts Press and the "OP" logo are trademarks belonging to Outskirts Press, Inc.

PRINTED IN THE UNITED STATES OF AMERICA

The Skinny On:
CREDIT CARDS
How to Win the Credit Card Game

The Skinny On:
CREDIT CARDS
How to Win the Credit Card Game

Jim Randel

Published by Clover Leaf Publishing, LLC

Copyright © 2008 by Jim Randel

ISBN: 978-0-9818935-4-9
Library of Congress Control Number: 2008939251

Editor: Leslie Greene
Illustration: Malinda Nass
Cover Design: Russell Zolan

ATTENTION:

Quantity discounts are available to
your company, educational organization or club.

For additional information, contact:
Donna Hardy (203) 222-6295 or visit our website:
www. jimrandel.com

"I also want to hear about the terms of the credit cards. The interest rates. I know my colleagues before said 'shame on the credit card companies'. I want to say 'hooray' for some of the credit card companies. They have single-handedly put the Mafia out of the business of making loans at usurious rates."

Congressman Gary Ackerman
New York, Fifth District
Committee on Financial Services
107th Congress, March 2003

The Skinny On™

Welcome to a new series of publications entitled **The Skinny On™**, a progression of drawings (stick people), dialogue and text intended to convey information in a concise fashion.

Most nonfiction books are 200 pages or more. Why? Because that is what worked 100 years ago. The problem is that people have less time to read than they did 100 years ago, and there is a lot more to read than there was 100 years ago.

The real substance in most nonfiction books can be conveyed in far fewer pages. We believe that less is more. As first said by French scholar Blaise Pascal in the 17th century when writing to an associate: "Sorry for the length of this letter, it would have been much shorter had I had more time."

We invest the time for you. We do all the reading. We then summarize and synthesize it for you.

In learning any subject, there are hundreds, maybe thousands of bits of information you need to absorb. In writing our books, we address the most important points a reader needs to learn about a given topic. Once you have read a "skinny" book, you will have a good understanding of a specific subject. Our bibliography identifies suggestions for further reading, if you are so inclined.

Although minimalist in design, drawing and verbiage, we take our message very seriously. Please do not confuse format with content. The time you invest reading our book will be paid back to you many times over.

INTRODUCTION

WOW! What a big topic – credit cards. That little piece of plastic (3.370" x 2.125") that has generated incredible convenience, heartache and commentary.

We take on this subject with humility. We realize the challenge in trying to educate people about credit cards in a short, synthesized book. Yet after months of writing and rewriting, we calculate that we've identified the 100 or so most important points you need to know – and they are all in our story.

First point, nobody stood up and asked the banks to invent credit cards. In fact, when they first appeared on a grand scale (1958), it was because the Bank of America put thousands of credit cards into the hands of the residents of one Southern California city. Here is how author Joe Nocera described it:

"America began to change on a mid-September day in 1958, when the Bank of America dropped its first 60,000 credit cards on the unassuming city of Fresno, California … a mass mailing of cards: a 'drop' … **There had been no outward yearning among the residents of Fresno for such a device, nor even the dimmest awareness that such a thing was in the works. It simply arrived one day, with no advance warning, as if it had dropped from the sky.***"*

> *A Piece of the Action: How the Middle Class Joined the Money Class*

In the ensuing 50 years, the credit card has, of course, become part of our lives. There are now about **700 million** active cards in the United States, that's 2 cards for every man, woman and child in our country. Total credit card debt is about **$1 trillion**, and it is estimated that the average U.S. household using credit cards has about $9,000 in card debt.

You are about to read the story of Billy and Beth, a typical U.S. couple, as they struggle with the use (and abuse) of their credit cards.

FOREWORD

As of the writing of this book in 2009, the credit card industry is in flux.

1. Due to a very difficult economy, defaults (when a cardholder stops paying what is due), and charge-off's (when a credit card issuer assumes the card holder is never going to pay) are higher than they have been in decades.

2. As a result, credit card issuers are cutting back on offerings, raising rates, closing cards, reducing card limits, contracting grace periods and increasing minimum payments. What is a bit frightening is that a unilateral action by a credit card issuer, e.g. lowering your credit line, can hurt your FICO score (to be explained) even if you have done nothing wrong. We will discuss these points in the pages ahead.

3. What's more, as a result of an enormous consumer groundswell against certain card issuers' lending and operating protocols, the Federal Reserve, which regulates U.S. lending, in December, 2008 adopted dramatic and substantive regulations to protect card holders. These regulations dictate how interest rates can be raised, when and how penalty fees can be applied, and how payments must be applied to balances. These regulations will become effective July, 2010. These regulations will be discussed in the pages ahead.

4. And, in September of 2008, the United States House of Representatives passed a bill titled "The Credit Cardholders Bill of Rights." This bill was never passed in the Senate but, with a new Administration and Congress, it has a good chance of becoming a law soon. We will discuss the provisions of this proposed law in our book.

Our goal is to educate you. We believe that if you understand the rules of the game and the principles of credit card use (and potential abuse), then the decisions you make about credit and debt will hopefully be good ones.

If you would like a free summary of the new credit card regulations, please go to our website at www.jimrandel.com.

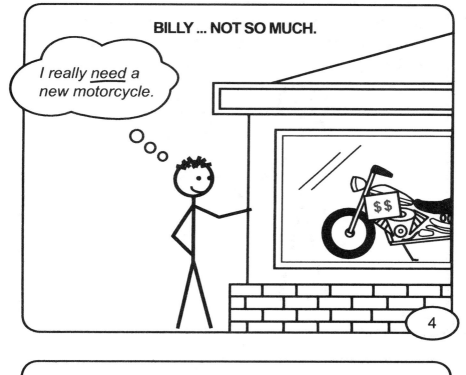

BILLY ... NOT SO MUCH.

I really <u>need</u> a new motorcycle.

BETWEEN THEM, THEY HAVE 13 CREDIT CARDS ...
BETH HAS THREE AND BILLY HAS TEN.

"The bill looks fine. Just give me a minute or two to figure out which credit card to use."

YOU MIGHT BE INTERESTED TO LEARN THAT ABOUT 14% OF U.S. CARDHOLDERS HAVE MORE THAN 10 CARDS.

75% OF U.S. FAMILIES HAVE AT LEAST ONE CREDIT CARD.

6

ONE MORNING

"Billy, we need to talk – we're accumulating a lot of credit card debt."

Uh-oh.

7

8

9

That brief encounter reveals a lot about how people get into credit card trouble.

Billy just doesn't like to think about spending, budgets or debts. He believes that's what tomorrow is for.

Billy and Beth have very different "**financial blueprints**."

What is a financial blueprint?

Author T. Harv Eker writes about "financial blueprints" in his book, *Secrets of the Millionaire Mind*. Eker's book helps people understand how they think about money … and why.

Much of how each of us relates to money and debt comes from our upbringing.

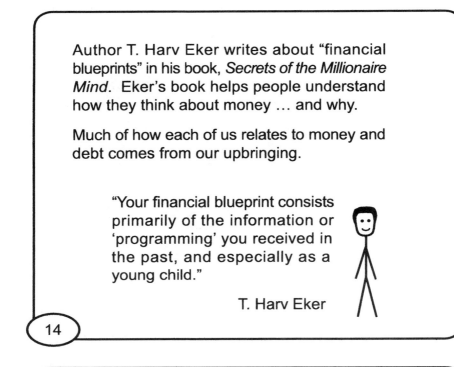

"Your financial blueprint consists primarily of the information or 'programming' you received in the past, and especially as a young child."

T. Harv Eker

LITTLE BILLY

"Carpe diem, my son. Life is meant to be lived!"

Have you had enough
of the platitudes?

We have obviously oversimplified the way children learn about money. It is not just what children <u>hear</u> from their parents.

More likely, it is what a young person sees and experiences ... those influences in his or her young life that impacted views about earning, spending and saving.

The point is that as adults we need to reflect upon how we think about money … about debt … about our own earning power and need for safety. In doing so, by bringing awareness to the subject, we improve our ability to manage our finances.

Oftentimes, successful people achieve not in spite of their upbringing but rather because of it.

In many stories, financial difficulties in childhood are the impetus for significant achievement later in life.

I can give you a good example of this point.

One of the best-known advisors on financial matters is Suze Orman. I have never met her, but she seems quite sincere in her desire to help people get on top of their money issues.

Here is an excerpt from her book, *The 9 Steps to Financial Freedom:*

"When I was very young, I had already learned that the reason my parents seemed so unhappy wasn't that they didn't love each other; it was that they never had quite enough money even to pay the bills. In our house money meant tension,worry and sorrow."

Ms. Orman's financial blueprint was formed at any early age. Money needs caused tension, worry and sorrow. So, as an adult, Ms. Orman has done what she can to provide for her own financial security, and that of the many people who follow her teachings.

Suze Orman

Before we go any further, take a few moments to reflect on your own "financial blueprint."

How important is money to you?

Is the need for money just a nuisance that must be handled so you can lead the life you want?

Or is it an integral part of the fabric of you? Is it a big part of your self-esteem?

How do you feel about savings? Will you ever feel comfortable that you have enough?

Are you constantly worrying about money? Do you believe that more money will make you happier?

There are, of course, no right or wrong answers to these questions. But thinking about them may help you understand how you feel about credit cards and debt.

Please put this book down for a minute or two and reflect on how your attitudes about money, debt and savings were formed.

As Harv Eker suggests, once you understand your "financial blueprint," you are better able to make good financial decisions.

Billy realizes that he cannot put Beth off forever. He knows that she is getting upset with him.

"Statistics show that the number one cause of all relationship breakups is money. The biggest reason behind fights people have about money is not the money itself, but the mismatch of their 'financial blueprints.'"

T. Harv Eker

And so Billy and Beth have a candid discussion.

Beth speaks to her fears about never having enough money,

and Billy reveals how buying things helps him feel good about himself.

BILLY AND BETH REALIZE THAT THEY NEED A BETTER UNDERSTANDING OF HOW CREDIT CARDS WORK.

Beth agrees to do the homework.

Beth finds that there are many books written about credit cards.

She feels overwhelmed!

And that, of course, is the exact reason why we've written *The Skinny on Credit Cards.*

Although Billy graduated from Harvard, he didn't learn much about real-world topics ... like credit cards. Unfortunately, very few U.S. high schools or colleges teach even basic financial principles.

*"Tens of thousands of students ... **learn the hard way** the pitfalls of misusing their credit cards – that colorful and friendly plastic which was irresponsibly pitched to them on registration day with offers of free candy, T-shirts, and beer mugs."*

Forever in Your Debt, Harvey Z. Warren

32

"I think it's time for me to make an appearance. I hope you don't think I'm butting in."

33

"Billy, you are a credit card issuer's dream … you occasionally pay late – earning them profitable late fees – and you always carry a balance… earning them lots of interest. You are what is called in credit card lingo a 'revolver' – you keep rolling over your debt and never pay it down."

IN THE TERMINOLOGY OF THE CREDIT CARD ISSUERS, SOMEONE WHO PAYS OFF THEIR BALANCE IN FULL EVERY MONTH IS A "DEADBEAT."

THE MEDIAN BALANCE ON A U.S. CREDIT CARD (WHICH MEANS THAT 50% OF CARD HOLDERS HAVE MORE AND 50% HAVE LESS) IS $2,200.

"I know this is confusing … in fact the credit card companies like it that way…. Here, this may help."

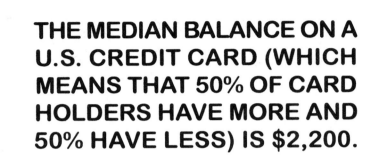

"Beth, we don't own a blackboard. Where'd that come from?"

???

50

Stick people books™ was inspired by the popular Japanese writing style known as manga. Manga books are illustrated, with a story line and dialogue. There is, at times, a moderator who jumps in and out of the story and with whatever accessories he wants, e.g. a blackboard.

"What a strange looking couple!"

How Billy and Beth might look in a manga book.

51

"It is really important that you understand how credit cards work. A credit card is nothing more than a way to borrow money.

You present the card to a merchant and your account is instantly contacted. In just seconds, your credit card company says 'OK' or 'Not OK' to your purchase.

If the credit card company says 'OK,' it loans you the money so that you can make the purchase. Nothing confusing there."

"What at times gets confusing is what happens once money is loaned to you.

Let's start with the basics:

#1: You will have time (depending on when in your billing cycle you make a purchase) between the date when you use your card (and get a loan), and the date when you get a bill.

#2: If you pay the bill (loan) in full when it is due (the 'due date'), you owe no interest.

#3: If you don't pay the bill in full, you will pay interest on that portion of the bill you do not pay off.

#4. The rate or amount of interest you pay is very important.

#5: What you are required to pay every month is called the 'minimum payment.'

#6: If you don't pay the minimum payment by the due date, bad things happen.

#7. When you use your card for anything but purchases of goods or services, there are additional fees.

I need to spend just one minute on each of these points."

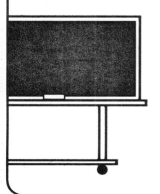

#1: The credit card companies send you a bill once a month. This bill lists all your charges. You should have at least two weeks ("**grace period**") from the date you receive your bill to the date when your payment must be received ("**due date**"). If you are going to be away for an extended period, call the card company and ask them to e-mail your bill to you. Not receiving the bill is no excuse.

You must be sure the card company **receives** your payment by the **due date**. Some card companies have **cutoff times** so that a check received at say noon on the due date might not be considered timely.

Explore paying your bill online.

#2: If you can pay 100% of your bill, do that. Then you will not pay any interest to the credit card company. About one-third of all U.S. cardholders pay their bill in full every month.

The term "**float**" is used to describe the period between the date you use your card and the date when payment is due. If you pay your bill in full every month, this float is a real convenience.

#3: If you don't pay the amount of your bill in full when it is due, the portion you don't pay is called your "**balance**." The credit card companies make money by charging you interest on your balance.

For example, let's say you charge $500 to your credit card during the month of June. On July 1 you get your bill and your due date is July 15. On July 15 you pay $100 of your bill. Your **balance** is $400; and starting on July 16, the credit card charges you interest on the $400 you still owe them.

In addition, if you carry a **balance**, your credit card company starts charging you interest on any new expenditures you make from the day you make them, i.e. no float.

#4: The rate or amount of interest you pay is a big deal. If you are carrying a balance, you want to know the **Annual Percentage Rate (APR)** you are being charged by the credit card company for the right to use their money (i.e. the loan).

The average APR in the U.S. today is about 14%.

Note that you can be charged different APRs for different uses you make of your card. We will discuss this again later in the book.

#5: The credit card company wants you to pay some portion of your bill every month – but it is a very small portion (usually about 2% of the amount of your bill). The amount they want you to pay is called the "**minimum payment**."

Paying just the **minimum payment** every month is a prescription for trouble, which we will discuss a little later. As you have read, Beth and Billy will need almost seven years to pay off their credit card balance if they cut up their cards right now, and make only the minimum payment every month.

#6: Credit card companies have no sense of humor if they do not receive your payment on time.

If you are late with a payment (the credit card company receives it after the due date), you will be hit with a "**late fee**," usually about $35-$40. Sometimes you can get these fees waived (reversed) if you have been a good customer and you call the credit card company.

In addition, if you are late, your APR will most likely spike upward to what is called a "**default rate**." A default rate is the APR charged on your balance when you have made mistakes. You won't like the default rate, it is usually about 16 points higher than the APR you were paying.

#7: The credit card companies are pretty ingenious when it comes to finding ways to charge you.

If you use your card for a purchase that will put your balance over your **credit line** (your maximum borrowing power on that card), you will get charged an **over-the-limit fee** (usually $35-$40).

If you use your card for a cash advance, there is typically a fee equal to 3% of the money advanced, and the interest on this money is often billed at a different APR than you are being charged on your balance. There are also fees for **balance transfers** (discussed later), and the use of your card overseas.

BACK TO BILLY, BETH, AND JIM

"Now that you understand the basics, I can explain why it will take you about seven years to pay off your credit card debt.

First, let me ask you a question:

Do either of you know what Albert Einstein called the most powerful force in the universe?"

"Nuclear fission?"

"Good guess, Beth, but no. It is something called '**compound interest**.'

Compound interest is the **earning of interest on interest**. Let me give you an example.

If you invest $1,000 in a savings account that is earning you 5% in interest, by the end of one year, you will have earned $50 in interest.

OK, now how much in interest will your account earn in the next year?"

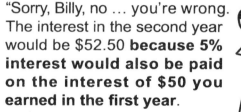

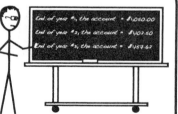

"$50 ...
that's easy."

"Sorry, Billy, no ... you're wrong. The interest in the second year would be $52.50 **because 5% interest would also be paid on the interest of $50 you earned in the first year**.

Then, in the third year, the interest earned on the account would be $55.12.

Here is the math:

> End of year #1, the account = $1,050.00
> End of year #2, the account = $1,102.50
> End of year #3, the account = $1,157.62

And so on. And in about 11 more years, your $1,000 investment will total $2,000."

"Now here's a short trick for helping you understand compound interest. It's called '**The Rule of 72**.'

If you want to know how fast your money will double in any particular investment with a fixed rate of return, divide the return you are earning into the number 72, and the result is the number of years it will take your money to double.

So, for example, if you invest $1,000 in an account earning 8%, then in 9 years ... 72 divided by 8 ... your account will be worth $2,000."

"That's cool."

"Unfortunately, the power of compound interest can also work against you. That is why the credit card companies make so much money.

Let's say you owe a credit card company $1,000 and they are earning 15% interest (the APR) on your debt. Do either of you want to guess how long it will take before you actually owe them $2,000 including the interest?"

"Well, Jim, I am thinking that the Rule of 72 works in this example, too. So, I would guess about 5 years ... 72 divided by 15 = 4.8."

"Great analysis, Beth, but unfortunately, wrong. It's actually quicker than that. You see The Rule of 72 assumes that interest is being added on interest **at the end of every year**. But, the credit card companies are smarter than that. They compound interest on interest **every day**. As a result they are required by law to tell you your **average daily interest rate**. In your case (15% APR), it is .04% (.0004)."

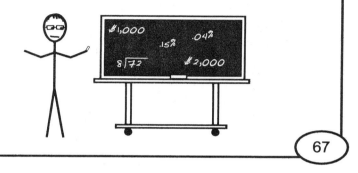

"I don't want to spend any more time on the math, but here is the point:

Every day you owe your credit card company money, they are earning interest **not just** on the sums you charged **but also** on the interest they earned on that sum in the preceding day or days. In other words, the interest you owe them is compounding … getting larger and larger every day.

That is a big reason why it will take you almost seven years to pay off your debt by making just the minimum payment."

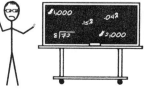

"Jim, maybe you should stop saying that ... Billy gets very tense when money is discussed."

"I'm sorry, Beth, but there is one more point that I need to make.

When you carry a balance on your credit cards, there is no longer an interest-free period between the date of a purchase and the date your payment is due. In other words, you start paying interest *the minute* a new purchase is made. I'm sorry to say, Billy, that you are already paying interest on that new motorcycle jacket you bought this morning."

Billy should not be too hard on himself.

Yes, he made some poor decisions. He did not control his spending. He did not budget.

But now he needs to move forward and take positive steps in an all-out effort to resolve his and Beth's difficulties.

Life is a series of steps and missteps.

As one who has studied successful people for many years, I have learned that they do not dwell on their missteps. They acknowledge their mistakes, resolve never to repeat them, and then immediately start making plans to remedy the situation.

Billy now needs to learn what his and Beth's options are to get on top of their credit card debt.

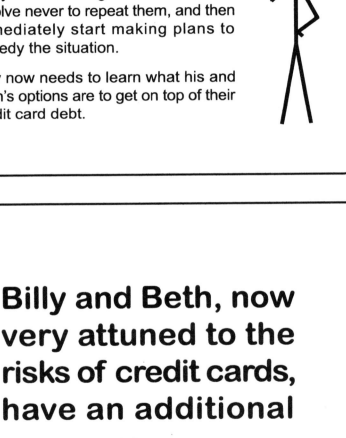

Billy and Beth, now very attuned to the risks of credit cards, have an additional concern:

THEIR 18-YEAR-OLD SON, JAKE.

JAKE IS A FRESHMAN IN COLLEGE.

It is legal for an 18-year old to get a credit card. And credit card marketers are aggressive in their efforts to put cards in the hands of young adults, especially college students.

"(T)he most profitable niche of the credit card market features consumers without jobs – college students. The credit card industry is aggressively marketing easy credit on campus … to young adults whose credit card morals are being shaped by the credit card 'carrot' with little knowledge of the proverbial collection 'stick' …"

Credit Card Nation, Robert Manning

In other words, young adults can be very susceptible to credit card marketers – leading to debt problems at any early age.

BILLY AND BETH ARE RIGHT TO BE WORRIED ABOUT JAKE.

As the credit card marketers well know, many young adults are anxious to be free of the parents' financial oversight.

Of course, it is not just young adults who are vulnerable to credit card marketing. All of us, whatever our age, are susceptible to the genius of the card marketing gurus.

The card companies spend hundreds of millions of dollars a year not just to get you to select their card over others **but also** to induce you to use it (over and over again). Many commentators are critical of card marketers – who they see as pushing people to take on debt.

"What has changed is the marketing of credit, the notion that credit is not a tool but a lifestyle. The financial industry spends vast sums of money spreading the myth that debt is good ... that wealth is spending, not saving, and that there will always be more credit...."

Maxed Out: Hard Times in the Age of Easy Credit
James Scurlock

"Those who go a borrowing, also go a sorrowing."

Ben Franklin

The great American thinker and leader Ben Franklin would probably agree with those who call credit cards "financial junk food."

Jake is making a basic mistake: He is assuming that if a credit card issuer is willing to give him a credit card, someone made a calculation that he had the ability to pay back any debt he incurred.

Unfortunately, that is not how credit card companies work, especially when it comes to young adults.

In his book, *Forever in Your Debt*, Harvey Z. Warren explains:

"Just because they send you the money, or offer you the credit, does not mean you have earned it, or need it, or should use it.

In the world of credit card marketing … it is easier and cheaper to mail credit cards by the tens of millions and clean up a financial disaster with a few customers, than to do the hard and labor-intensive work of genuinely qualifying all of the customers."

Or, as one credit card executive told me (in confidence):

"We figure that the great percentage of young adults will find a way to pay us. It is too expensive to carefully prequalify all applicants, so we just extend lots and lots of cards."

Jake has a point. He is old enough to join the Armed Forces. He **should be able** to handle a couple of credit cards.

The problem is that we, as a country, have not done a good job preparing our young people for a very smart and well-armed credit card industry.

Billy and Beth now realize that it was their responsibility to teach Jake basic financial principles. They hope it's not too late.

"Next time we see Jim Randel we should ask him to write a book about credit cards that we can buy for Jake."

"Great idea!"

94

95

"In the meantime, let's learn all we can about credit cards ... both for ourselves and for what we can teach Jake."

"Definitely! And, by the way, Beth, I'm sorry for getting us in this mess."

Hey, good for Billy and Beth. They are now moving in a forward direction – taking responsibility for their mistakes and starting the process of learning, looking for solutions to their problem.

As we go down that path with them, let's review exactly where they are:

Billy and Beth are in debt to credit card issuers for a total amount of $25,000. For the past year, they paid just the minimum payment ($500/mo.) and were late one time. Assuming they cut up their cards right now, it will take them almost 7 years to get out of debt.

Fortunately for Billy and Beth there are steps they can take to pay down their debt more quickly. My job is to help them understand their options.

"Billy, there's only so much reading I can do ... Would you object if I call that Randel guy and see if he will help us?"

"No, Beth, I guess that's OK."

102

103

I stole that phrase from author Harvey Z. Warren (actually, he told me I could use it) because it explains so well how people get into debt … and can't get out.

About twenty-five years ago, credit card companies were requiring monthly minimum payments that were about 5% of card balances. Then along came a smart credit card consultant named **Andrew Kahr**, who convinced his clients to lower minimum payments.

Kahr was very shrewd. He knew that the less that people were required to pay every month, the more they would use their card, and the longer it would take to reduce debt. In both cases, his card company clients were making more interest.

Kahr also understood psychology. He knew that people who were making the required payment would believe that they were acting prudently.

Given the size of some people's balances, there were times when a minimum payment was not even covering interest due the card company. Card companies are now required to bill at least an amount that covers the interest due.

The reality is that by inducing people to pay just the 2% minimum, credit card companies were helping people dig themselves into deeper and deeper holes.

"No, not yet … just keep digging."

"I think I hit bottom."

To see a rare interview of Andrew Kahr (the guy is kind of secretive) and an excellent video about credit cards – a PBS special called "The Secret Life of Credit Cards" – go to:

http://www.pbs.org/wgbh/pages/frontline/ shows/credit/view/

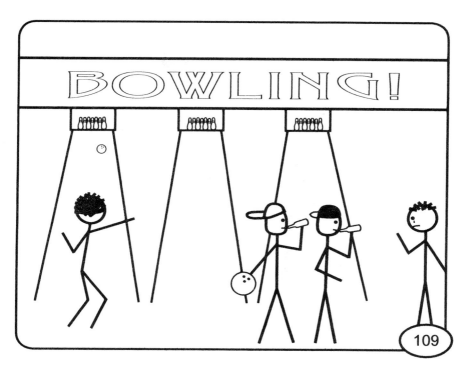

Good for Billy. He is trying to make changes to find additional money for debt reduction.

An author named David Bach has created a series of successful books around the idea that by saving small sums every day, one can use that money (with compound interest) to build up a healthy net worth.

You may have heard of his idea, "The Latte Factor":

"how we dribble away what should be our fortunes on small things…."

The Automatic Millionaire

"That's great, Billy ... and by paying $750 a month instead of $500, you can pay off your debt in 44 months instead of 79!"

$25,000
15%
$720/month
44 months

"Wow, we can shave three years off."

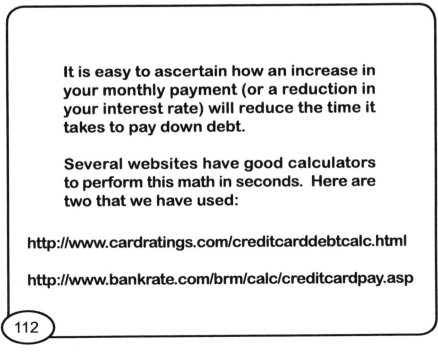

It is easy to ascertain how an increase in your monthly payment (or a reduction in your interest rate) will reduce the time it takes to pay down debt.

Several websites have good calculators to perform this math in seconds. Here are two that we have used:

http://www.cardratings.com/creditcarddebtcalc.html

http://www.bankrate.com/brm/calc/creditcardpay.asp

OK, thanks.

Thousands of years ago, lenders were not even allowed to earn interest on money they loaned to others. But this system only worked if all borrowers paid back a loan when the lender wanted it. Unfortunately, that is not human nature.

Eventually lenders were allowed to charge borrowers a fee for using the lender's money. This fee is called interest.

Still, even though lenders could charge interest, there were laws about **how much** interest they could charge. A rate in excess of what was considered reasonable was termed "**usurious.**" Lending beyond the lending limit is called "**usury.**"

Most States have laws against usury – generally any interest rate above 18%. Credit card issuers outsmarted the system by locating their credit card operations in States with no usury laws – like South Dakota or Delaware. That is why credit card issuers can charge rates as high as 30% and above.

"The key for any borrower is to keep the interest rate on his or her debt as low as possible. The lower the rate, the less the borrower has to pay the lender, and the greater the opportunities a borrower has to make good use of the borrowed funds.

"Credit card users should always be on the lookout for ways to lower their interest rate. In that regard, I have two suggestions."

"Wonderful ... what are they?"

116

"First I was thinking you might be getting a little weary with all the money talk. So, how about a joke? Want to hear my favorite?"

"OK!"

117

"Just as I suspected ... typical language: Your credit card issuer can change your rate whenever it feels like it."

132

"Here is the language that gives card companies enormous discretion to change your rate: '*At any time, we may add, delete or change any term of this Agreement unless we told you that we would not*.'"

"But, Jim, as I recall, my application indicated what our interest rate would be."

133

"Yes, Beth, the application is required to do that. But, again, you need to read the fine print. Your application also happens to say:

'In the future, we may increase your APRs if market conditions change.'"

The credit card industry is very good at meeting the terms of the law, right at its edges. In other words, while they may abide by the strict letter of the law, they do not do all that they can to help credit card applicants and holders understand the terms and conditions of credit card usage.

For example a section of the U.S. Truth-in-Lending Law requires that credit card offers explain in an identifiable area the basic terms of the credit card. Because this law was introduced by Senator Charles Schumer, this part of the marketing material is called the "Schumer Box."

"Look at the typical Schumer box below. Is that helpful to you?"

ANNUAL PERCENTAGE RATE (APR) for purchases	0% (0.00000% daily periodic rate) through your 07/2009 billing period. After that, a variable rate, currently equal to **8.9%** (0.02438% daily periodic rate).
Other **APRs**	Balance transfer APR: Same as for purchases. Cash advance APR: a variable rate, currently equal to 22.9% (0.06274% daily periodic rate). Default APR: A variable rate, currently equal to 23.9% (0.06548% daily periodic rate). See explanation below.
Variable rate information	Your purchase APR may vary quarterly. The rate will be determined by adding 3.9% to the Prime rate. * Rate in effect 10/01/2008. Your balance transfer APR may vary quarterly. The rate will be determined by adding 3.9% to the Prime rate. * Rate in effect 10/01/2008. Your cash advance APR may vary quarterly. The rate will be determined by adding 17.9% to the Prime rate. * Rate in effect 10/01/2008. Your default APR may vary monthly. The rate will be determined by adding 19.9% to the Prime rate. * Rate in effect 10/01/2008.

Can You Increase My APRs? Your variable APRs can go up or down as the Prime rate goes up or down. Your introductory APRs may expire and increase to your non-introductory APRs if your payment is received late (3 or more days after your payment due date). We may increase your APRs to the Default APR disclosed above if your payment is received late twice within any 12 billing periods. If we increase your APRs to the Default APR, we will return you to our non-introductory if you make at least the minimum payment on time for 12 consecutive billing periods. In the future, we may increase your APRs if market conditions change. If we increase your APRs for any reason other than an increase in the Prime rate or if you paid late as disclosed above, we will notify you in writing of your options in advance, including the right to opt out.

What About Any Other Terms Of My Account? We may change any other terms of your account, other than APRs, at any time. If we change any of these terms, we will notify you in writing of your options in advance, including the right to opt out of certain changes.

"Even my roommate in college couldn't understand that!"

"I don't know, Billy. That Bill Gates was pretty smart."

I think the Schumer Box is totally confusing.

By indicating the specifics of how the APR is calculated, the inference is that the card company cannot just change the rate whenever it wants.

Some card companies even use the term "fixed rate." That just means that the APR is not tied to another rate which can move up and down with changes in the economy. It does not mean that the card company cannot change a "fixed" rate.

You will often see reference to a "prime rate" in Schumer boxes. The "prime rate" is the rate that commercial lenders charge their best customers. It can change daily.

I get angry when I talk about this stuff. If there are going to be laws that require disclosure, the laws and the disclosures should be in plain language.

Here is what the Schumer Box should say:

"We, your credit card company, can do whatever the heck we want. So, make your payments on time. Don't borrow past your credit limit. Keep your credit rating as strong as possible. Then, maybe we won't change your interest rate."

I'LL BET YOU UNDERSTAND THAT!!

140

"Basically, issuers may change your rate at any time for any reason."

The Credit Card Guidebook,
Bill Hardekopf

141

For now you need to understand that, except for specific offers (e.g. "0% for 12 months"), credit card companies have great leeway in changing your APR.

And, even with specific offers, if your payment is late by even one day, the deal is off. Your credit card issuer can then apply a "default rate," which today (on average) is 16 percentage points higher than the APR you were paying.

Many people feel that the credit card issuers have been too aggressive in trying to make money, an example being their unilateral ability to change rates – pretty much whenever they feel like it.

In 2008 the Federal Reserve Board (in charge of all U.S. lending) asked consumers for comments about their credit card. The Fed received an unprecedented number of comments (about 60,000 in 3 months) – the great majority of which were critical of card companies.

And so, in December of 2008 the Fed adopted regulations as to how credit card companies can operate. These regulations take effect in July, 2010.

Here is a summary of some of the new regulations, defining what card issuers can and cannot do:

1. During the first year you have a card, they cannot raise your rate unless you are 30 days late. After the first year, they can raise your rate without the 30-day requirement but only if they give you 45 days advance notice.

2. They cannot apply a new rate to existing balances unless you are 30 days late.

3. They cannot hit you with a late fee unless there is at least 21 days between when the bill is mailed and the due date.

4. When applying a payment to a card with differing APR's, they must either apply the entire payment to the item with the highest interest rate or, they must allocate the payment proportionately.

For example, if your card includes a balance transfer of $2,000 at a 0% APR and a cash advance of $4,000 at a 20% APR, the card issuer must either apply all of your payment to the $4,000 (higher interest rate item) or, 1/3 to the $2,000 owed and 2/3 to the $4,000 owed. This is much fairer than the practice today whereby many card issuers apply your entire payment to the $2,000 owed, i.e. they don't want to reduce the $4,000 (20% interest).

If you are confused, please e-mail your question to: info@randmediaco.com.

Since the new regulations wont' take effect until mid-2010, you may be asking yourself whether you have any recourse, any ability to fight back against rate increases.

First, be aware that current law requires that a card holder receive at least 15 days' advance notice before a rate increase can be imposed. This is not much protection, but it is something.

Second, a card company cannot unilaterally change the rate on an introductory offer (e.g., "0% for 12 months") unless you are late or do something wrong.

Finally, remember that the "squeaky wheel sometimes gets the grease." Don't be afraid to call your card company and challenge a rate increase. Sometimes proposed increases can be reversed.

One final point about credit card companies changing your rate and other card terms.

Oftentimes these changes come in nondescript looking envelopes that can be confused for junk mail. If you accidentally throw away one of these letters, doing so might cost you if, for example, the letter indicated a change in your grace period or credit limit, and you unknowingly paid late, or went over your borrowing limit.

I hate junk mail.

A lot of people don't read materials provided to them by credit card issuers. In large part, this is because these materials are too confusing and too long.

In fact, in a recent survey, ¾ of Americans polled indicated that "complexity and confusion" have played a major role in the current financial crisis and 63% believe that financial institutions "**intentionally make things complicated to hide risks or keep people in the dark**."

One third of those polled indicated they "sometimes" or "never" read credit card applications.

Survey conducted by Siegel and Gale

We at **The Skinny On™** believe that credit card companies could do a much better job educating consumers. We believe that credit card issuers must work hard at preparing **simple, clear and easy-to-understand applications and agreements**.

Because of the large number of consumer complaints about credit cards, many of which relate to confusion over what issuers can and can't do, we expect to see a bill titled "**The Credit Cardholders Bill of Rights**," become law in 2009. This bill speaks to the need for "**clear**" explanations of account features, terms and pricing.

If this bill becomes law, our website will include a summary of the important provisions you need to know.

I CAN'T HELP MYSELF. I'M GETTING ON A SOAP BOX

"Gather around, friends: While some of what the credit card companies do is shabby, we do not have to take their money.

"Some credit card companies deserve criticism for letting their marketing and operational geniuses create protocols that trick or confuse people. But, my friends, we can win the credit card game. We can educate ourselves. We can lobby for changes in the law. We can take responsibility for our own actions. We can win this battle."

Do you know where the expression "speaking on a soap box" comes from?

Yes, of course. Starting in the 1800's in London, speakers would get on a box used for holding soap and start talking, talking, talking … holding court on any of a variety of subjects.

Can you think of the modern equivalent of speaking on a soap box?

How about **blogging**? Is not that the 21st century equivalent of someone climbing onto a soap box and talking, talking, talking??

Back To Our Story

"Wow, if credit card companies can change rates whenever they want to, I can certainly call them and *demand* that they lower my rates."

153

"Well, Billy, let's not use the word 'demand.' You can be forceful, but you should be polite. The person you initially speak with may not even have the authority to lower your rates. Always ask to speak with a supervisor and like everything else in life, be persistent. Don't lose your cool. Keep pressing until you get satisfaction or, until someone in authority tells you that a rate reduction is just not possible."

154

"Are there any special words we should use when asking for a rate reduction?"

"No special words, Beth. You can tell them that you need some assistance so that you can stay current with your debts. You should also tell them that you have offers from other cards at lower rates."

Author David Bach says, *"The fastest way to save money on your credit card debt is to … get your credit card company to lower the interest rate it charges you … when you are connected with a supervisor, tell him or her that a competing bank is offering you a much lower interest rate … unless he can match or beat the competitor's rate, you intend to transfer your balance to that competitor."*

Start Late, Finish Rich

This is a really important point to understand: unless you are a real problem, your credit card issuer **does not** want to lose you as a customer. The fact is that in most cases it costs a credit card company more to obtain a new customer than it loses by lowering an interest rate for an existing customer.

With the exception of one late payment (for which the issuer earned a $39 late fee), Billy and Beth have been steady customers. If Billy and Beth indicate that they have alternative card opportunities, some of their issuers may be willing to lower rates to match the other "offers" Billy and Beth have "received."

"Balance transfer cards usually have low rates for a set period of time. Upon paying a fee, you can transfer other card balances to the new card."

IMPORTANT POINTS ABOUT LOW-INTRODUCTORY-RATE TRANSFER CARDS

1. There is a fee to allow the transfer …usually about 3%.

2. The new card issuer will decide how much you can transfer … don't close an existing card until you know exactly how much you can put on the new card.

3. Low introductory rates go sky-high if you are ever late with a payment.

4. Low rates often do not apply to new charges … just the transferred balance.

5. If you do use this card for new charges, under current allocation-of-payment protocols, your payments will reduce the 0% balance portion of your bill before the higher-interest new charges.

Any questions so far?? We at **The Skinny On™** don't want you to think that since you purchased our book, we no longer have an interest in you. Any buyer of our book is **a life long friend**. So, if you have a question, please go to our website (www.jimrandel.com) and look at Frequently Asked Questions. If there is not an answer to your question, please e-mail me at www.jrandel@randmedia.com.

In other words, like it or not, you now have a new friend.

"Beth, these low-rate balance transfer cards sound great…let's start applying for these cards right away."

Yes, Billy, I am … and no reason for the sarcasm.

FICO is an acronym for the Fair Isaacs Corporation, a company that has developed an algorithm to measure people's creditworthiness.

> **ACRONYM**: a word made up of the first letters of several words
>
> **ALGORITHM**: mathematical formula
>
> **CREDITWORTHINESS**: likelihood of paying all obligations on time

FICO receives information from the three big credit reporting bureaus: Experian, Equifax and TransUnion. It then takes this information and produces a three-digit number: ranging from 300 at the low end to 850 at the top.

Your FICO score (sometimes called your credit score) is critical in determining the amount, type, and cost of credit you will be offered by lenders. In addition, prospective employers, insurance companies and even landlords will sometimes check your FICO score to get a sense of how reliable you are.

"#1: Your FICO score is theoretically a **predictor** of how you will pay your bills.

#2: Your FICO score is only **as accurate** as your credit report. There is an expression 'garbage in, garbage out.' FICO just provides the formula.

#3: Get a copy of your credit report right now. Each of the three big credit bureaus must give you your report once a year **for free**. Go to www.annualcreditreport.com.

#4: Read your credit report carefully. One study indicated that 25% of all credit reports have **mistakes** in them.

#5: If you find a mistake, contact the credit bureau immediately. There are **procedures** established by law for disputing a negative credit entry (or "**ding**").

#6: FICO is a formula that is applied differently by each of the three big credit bureaus. So you actually have three (similar) FICO scores. The median FICO score is 723. If your score is below 700, credit will cost you more than for those people with a score above 700.

#7: Credit reports are free **but not FICO scores**. Still, the cost to obtain your score is not much (+/- $10).

#8: Your FICO score is **constantly changing**. To keep on top of the information affecting your score, request your credit report (free) from one of the three big companies **every four months**.

#9: If you want to go to the horse's mouth to learn about the FICO scoring system, go to **www.myfico.com**, the site of the Fair Isaacs Corporation.

#10: The two most important factors to Fair Isaacs in producing your FICO score are: 1) your **current payment record**, and 2) your **ratio of debt to borrowing power**.

#11: Don't try to change your FICO score **overnight**. It usually takes a month or two.

#12: The quickest way to improve your FICO score is to reduce your debt so that your ratio (actual debt to available debt) is **30% or less**. In other words, pay down debt if you can.

#13: FICO does not like to see credit cards being used near their limit. If you can, transfer or pay down debt so that **no one card is maxed** out, or near its limit.

#14: FICO pays more attention to your **recent behavior** than past. With time even mistakes lose their scoring impact.

#15: If you want to stop using a card, that's great. Just **don't close it** … doing so lowers your debt-to-available debt ratio.

#16: Every time you apply for credit, and a potential **creditor pulls your credit report**, your FICO score can be impacted. If **you** obtain your own credit report, however, there is no impact on your FICO score.

#17: FICO likes **longevity** in borrowing relationships. Keep old accounts open. If your card company threatens to close a card because it has been inactive, use it occasionally.

#18: **Be wary** of any company that promises a quick boost to your credit score or, "instant" credit repair. No legitimate company can make these promises.

#19: **Identity theft** is very real and can have a big impact on your FICO score. To learn more go to www.ftc.gov/bcp/edu/microsites/idtheft/.

#20: Don't do stuff you would not otherwise do, **solely for purposes** of your FICO score. Do your best to be a responsible borrower, and a good number will ensue."

As you can see, I'm climbing back on my soap box.

There is something about the FICO scoring system that bothers me. It is too secretive. We really don't even know how accurate it is in predicting behavior.

I also don't like that Fair Isaacs forces consumers to pay to receive their FICO score. And, then sells monitoring services to keep an eye on changes in the score (mistakes?).

Some people believe that FICO is a mysterious system for rating people that has never proven to be accurate. No transparency. No free access. Too much upselling.

> *"Given all the problems with credit scoring, it's understandable that some people think the system is fatally flawed. Some of my readers tell me they're so angry about scoring … they've cut up their credit cards …."*
>
> *Your Credit Score*, Liz Pulliam Weston

"Here's some good news. If, by calling your card companies for lower rates and, by transferring some debt to a lower-rate card, you can bring the average APR on your cards down from 15% to say 10%, then the time it will take you to pay down your credit card debt drops from 44 months to 39 months!"

"Beth, I am getting excited. I feel that we can definitely do this."

"Billy, so do I."

That short exchange between Billy and Beth is really important. They have gone from very disillusioned to hopeful. That is a very important transition – people only give up when they believe there is no hope.

While some financial commentators suggest that people with debt on several credit cards (like Billy and Beth) pay down the **highest-rate card first**, which, of course, makes economic sense, others have a different point of view. Other authors and advisors suggest that card holders pay down the card with the **lowest balance first**. In this way a card holder can see results more quickly, giving him or her the impetus to keep working hard at paying down debt.

"(Paying off the card with the smallest balance) doesn't necessarily jibe with conventional wisdom that says you should first pay off the card with the highest interest rate. Yet by concentrating on extinguishing the smallest balance first, you see more quickly the fruits of your labor. That will keep you motivated."

The Wall Street Journal Personal Finance Book, Jeff P. Opdyke

"Jim, you mentioned that there were three points to your debt-reduction program."

"Yes, Billy, the last suggestion is to do whatever you can to find a chunk of money to immediately lower some of your card debt. Doing so will dramatically reduce the time it takes to get out of debt. I call this one: 'Big Chunk = Less Funk.'"

HERE ARE JIM'S SUGGESTIONS TO BILLY AND BETH:

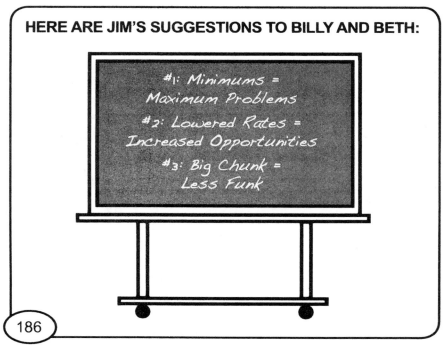

#1: Minimums = Maximum Problems

#2: Lowered Rates = Increased Opportunities

#3: Big Chunk = Less Funk

AND HERE'S A QUICK RECAP OF HOW THESE POINTS HELP ACCELERATE CREDIT CARD DEBT REDUCTION:

#1: By paying more than the minimum required payment every month, instead of just treading water, you chip away at the amount you owe.

#2: By lowering your APR, more of your monthly payment goes to debt reduction. Call your company and ask for lower rates based on competitive rates with other companies. Explore a balance transfer card.

#3: By making a lump-sum payment, you reduce total debt immediately, meaning that every successive monthly payment bites down on more and more debt.

"Well, I need to go now. Good luck."

Just for fun, while Billy and Beth are strategizing, I have prepared a little FICO-inspired quiz for you ... see if you can match up the left with the right ... answers are in the back of the book.

POP QUIZ

1) FIFO	A) Restaurant chain
2) DOJO	B) Real estate term
3) HILO	C) Singer
4) SOSO	D) Therefore
5) FIDO	E) Accounting term
6) KUDO	F) First name of famous gangster
7) HOJO	G) Vibe
8) LIDO	H) Martial arts studio
9) BONO	I) Dog in *Wizard of Oz*
10) NATO	J) Measurement of weight
11) VITO	K) Seaport in Hawaii
12) RICO	L) First name of famous designer
13) ERGO	M) Treaty organization
14) TOJO	N) Ordinary
15) TITO	O) Swimming pool in U.K.
16) MOJO	P) Honor
17) FSBO	Q) Legal statute
18) KILO	R) European dictator
19) TOTO	S) Japanese general
20) COCO	T) Billy and Beth's dog

189

"I'm excited, Beth. I feel we can get our debt down to 0. I went on a credit card calculator and if we get our average rate down to 10%, make monthly payments of $750, and find a $10,000 chunk like Jim said, we can pay all our debt in about 18 months."

"I'm excited too Billy, but where are we going to find $10,000?"

190

"Well, on Randel's website it talks about *thinking outside the box* to find whatever cash you can … so I have been thinking outside the box."

UH-OH.

191

Business arrangements among friends and family are always fraught with risk.

196

197

"I know you love your motorcycle, but if you sell it for say, $10,000, and use that money to reduce your credit card debt, with other ideas we've discussed you could pay off your debt in no time."

198

I hope that Billy and Beth understand why I am unwilling to loan them money. Believe me, I have been in these situations before and they often turn nice relationships sour. Billy, like many of us, needs to identify what is important to him right now.

One year ago, he used his credit card to buy a new motorcycle for $20,000. And since he and Beth have been making only minimum monthly payments, this purchase with interest compounding is a big part of their $25,000 debt.

I believe he should sell the bike. I realize that he loves it, but first and foremost he should get his financial house in order. Let's see what he decides.

199

I hope that you don't think it was pushy of me to suggest that Billy sell his motorcycle. After all, he was about to ask me for a loan.

Billy's decision to sell his motorcycle was painful for him. He got great pleasure from riding around on his Harley. And, perhaps that was more important to him than living debt-free. But, Billy and Beth were starting to struggle under the weight of their debt. And, given the economy today, we all need to face the reality of tough times ahead.

"If you care about financial security for yourself and your family ... you will not get there with wishful thinking or procrastination. You cannot sit this one out. ... The fact is that the new reality requires new strategies ... tactical actions to make sure you do not let the credit crisis knock you off course."

Suze Orman's 2009 ACTION PLAN: Keeping Your Money Safe and Sound

We at **The Skinny On™** are not anti-debt. We believe in the judicious use of debt. We believe that there are times when the ability to borrow can enhance your enjoyment of life.

"People borrow to smooth the timing of income and consumption over their lifetimes. ... There is no reason why anyone would want their level of consumption over time to track their income exactly. So, borrowing, including on credit cards, is a way of using future income to pay for immediate consumption. ... We value the present more than the future and are willing to pay to pull future consumption toward the present."

Paying with Plastic, Evans and Schmalensee

To be contrasted are authors and commentators who believe that debt is simply bad, bad, bad.

Here is a quote from a well-known, no-debt advocate, Dave Ramsey:

*"I remember a finance professor telling us that debt was a two-edged sword, which could cut **for you** like a tool but could also cut **into you** and bring harm. The myth has been sold that we should use OPM (debt), other people's money, to prosper.*

"The academic garbage is spread really thick on this issue…. My contention is that debt brings on enough risk to offset any advantage that could be gained through leverage … According to Proverbs 22:7: 'The rich rules over the poor, and the borrower is servant to the lender' …. I was confronted with this Scripture and had to make a conscious decision of who was right – my broke finance professor, who taught that debt is a tool, or God, who showed obvious disdain for debt."

The Total Money Makeover, Dave Ramsey

Dave Ramsey

"Gee guys, thanks, but I'm OK. I have two cards but each has a limit of only $500. I can't get into much debt."

STATE UNIVERSITY

207

Fortunately, Billy and Beth got to Jake before he could get into much trouble. Many credit card companies hook young adults (18 is the minimum age for a credit card) with easy credit, and then as debt is accumulated, keep upping their credit limit. By senior year, most college students have two or three credit cards with an average debt of $2,500. Eight percent of bankruptcies are the result of debt accumulated during college.

BIG POINT:

If you are the parent of a young adult, start talking to him or her about credit cards and debt!!

RIGHT NOW!!

I'm flattered that Billy and Beth asked me to meet with Jake and give him some points he needs to know about credit cards.

"Hi, Jake, I'm Jim Randel – a good friend of your mom and dad."

"They mentioned what a great friend you have been to our family ... thanks so much!"

Here is what I told Jake:

1. Don't sign a credit card application **just to get a free T-shirt**. Any application can affect your credit (FICO) score.

2. I do, however, **recommend getting a credit card** during college. Credit card expert, Liz Weston advises that "it will never be easier for you to get an unsecured credit card than while you're in school."

3. The cards offered on campus may not be the best deals available. **Shop around online**.

4. Your card should **not have an annual fee**.

5. Do not get a card which emphasizes **rewards**. These cards have more expensive terms and during college you should focus on low-cost cards.

6. Just because a credit card company is offering you a card does not mean it made a determination that you are able to pay off debt you incur. You are likely part of a **mass offering**.

7. You don't need more than **one credit card**.

8. If you are concerned about impulse spending, get a **debit ard** instead of a credit card. A debit card is backed (and limited) by the funds you have in your checking account.

9. Every time you reach for your credit card, **ask your-self** whether you can repay **what you are borrowing**. When? How?

10. In fact, I suggest wrapping a **rubber band** around your card which takes at least 10 seconds to remove. Use that time to reflect on whether you really need what you are buying.

11. If you carry a balance on your card, be very cautious about **card offers which increase your spending (borrowing) limit**. This is how people get into trouble.

12. You need to have a **basic understanding of how FICO works**. If you like, go to our website for periodic updates on changes in credit-scoring protocols.

13. How you handle credit and debt during college will affect your credit score and could impact post-college **employment opportunities** (one estimate: 1/3 of prospective employers check credit scores).

14. Start each school year with a **$0 balance**. If you carry a balance, use your school breaks to earn money and pay any card debt down to 0.

15. Enjoy yourself during college. It is a great time of life! Find joy in learning, meeting new people, exploring your interests and boundaries … **not in consumption**. There is plenty of time for that later.

"Thanks, Uncle Jim."

"And every month our payment is chipping away more debt."

Beth has just made a very important observation ... as you begin to pay down credit card debt, the amount of each payment that is needed to pay interest drops and the amount that goes toward debt reduction increases.

In other words, with each successive payment, you are paying down more and more debt.

Billy's comment that he "made a mistake" references the fact that cards with rewards benefits are usually more expensive (rates especially) than other cards and therefore should not be used by people who carry balances on their cards.

"Chapter 2. Show Me the Money! Credit Card Rebates. … Important! This Chapter is for people who pay off their balance in full each and every month. ***If you carry a balance – even on occasion – then move on to the next chapter.*** *Reward cards usually carry a higher interest rate than non-reward cards, and the interest you'll be charged will more than wipe out any rewards you might earn."*

How You Can Profit from Credit Cards, Curtis Arnold

BILLY AND BETH HAVE A GREAT TIME IN NIAGARA FALLS.

227

228

229

230

Good for Billy and Beth! We here at **The Skinny On™** are very happy for them. And, for you, we have prepared our list of the 15 Most Important Points to understand about credit cards.

By the way, I'm the one who bought Billy's motorcycle. He doesn't know. I overpaid, but so what? Life is for living.

15 ways to ensure your financial well being

OUR LIST OF THE 15 MOST IMPORTANT POINTS TO UNDERSTAND ABOUT CREDIT CARDS

——— 1 ———
Credit cards are a loan.

Credit cards are nothing more than a mechanism for borrowing money. If you can pay your balance off in full every month, you don't pay the card companies any interest, and the period of the loan is the time from when you make a purchase to the date when you have to make your monthly payment ("due date"). This is an interest-free period sometimes called a "float."

For most card holders, the loan extends beyond the due date, since they carry a balance.

The key to managing credit cards is understanding the terms of the credit card issuer loan.

As with any loan, you need to know:

1) Your interest rate;
2) The amount of your monthly payment;
3) When it is due;
4) How you make payment;
5) What happens if your payment is late;
6) What happens if you request an amount beyond your approved loan (credit line); and
7) How long it will take you to pay off your loan.

There is other information you should know, of course, but the above points are the most important.

— 2 —

Preapproved is
not prequalified.

Just because someone is willing to give you a loan
– a credit card – does not mean that person has
reviewed and analyzed your ability to repay the loan.

Some people tend to think that if they get a credit
card offer, someone has concluded there is an ability
to repay whatever is borrowed. But that's not how
it works.

In fact, oftentimes the issuance and approval of credit
cards, and determination of specific terms, is far from
scientific:

Credit Card Executives

———— 3 ————

Credit cards are going to be harder to get, and to keep.

Until recently, it was said that anyone who could fog a mirror could get a credit card. For those with a poor credit rating (FICO score), the terms might have been expensive, but credit cards were still available.

As of this writing in the spring of 2009, credit card issuers are nervous about the magnitude of defaults – that is, the number of people who are walking away from their credit card debt. As a result, the credit card issuers are:

1) Making it harder to get a card;
2) Raising required minimum payments;
3) Raising interest rates and other fees, what they call "risk profiling";
4) Lower credit limits; and
5) Canceling cards.

It is therefore more important than it has been in many years for you to maintain a good credit score, and meet all the terms and conditions of your existing credit cards.

Low monthly payments are not your friend.

Credit card issuers make money by lending you money and charging you interest.

They do not like people who pay off their monthly balance in full every month. They prefer people who make the minimum monthly payment and carry a balance. The higher your balance, the more they like you.

That is why credit card issuers make the monthly minimum payment so low. The less you pay every month, the higher your balance.

Those who pay only the required minimum are paying very little toward the amount they owe, and are digging themselves a hole. Paying a monthly minimum of 2%, is a prescription for many, many years of debt payment.

The credit card agreement is very one-sided.

If you can understand the credit card contract (usually about 20 pages), I want to hire you immediately. I'm not sure for what … it's just that you must be very, very smart.

Elizabeth Warren, a professor of contract law at Harvard Law School, notes that she cannot understand the credit card agreement.

Basically, however, here is what you really need to know:

IT IS TOTALLY ONE-SIDED.

First of all, if you slip up even a little bit, e.g. paying late or accidentally exceeding your credit line, all sorts of bad things are going to happen. Your grace period may shorten (the time between the date of your bill and the due date), your interest rate may spike upward, you will be hit with excessive fees, and your cell phone will be run over by a car (just kidding about the cell phone).

Even if you don't slip up, the credit card agreement gives your company enormous flexibility as to raising rates any time it wants. With the exception of introductory period rates (e.g., "2.99% for 12 months"), your credit card issuer can pretty much raise your rate at any time. **Not exactly a two-sided agreement**.

Make a budget!!

How can you control your life and use debt responsibly if you do not know exactly what you are spending?

Making a budget means nothing more than sitting down with a sheet of paper and identifying how much you have coming in every month, and how much you have going out. If you have more going out than coming in, you are operating "at a loss". The spread between what comes in and what goes out is often bridged with credit card borrowing.

Credit card borrowing is not in and of itself a bad thing. It allows you to cover shortfalls and enjoy products/services in advance of your ability to pay for them. But, where credit cards get dangerous is when people use them indiscriminately.

There are many sites online that offer you budget-making tools. Here are a couple of suggestions:

www.mint.com
www.myspendingplan.com
www.mybudgetplanner.com

"A budget is just a method for worrying about your expenditures **before** you make them … rather than **after**."

Credit cards are deliberately designed to make borrowing very, very easy.

It is not an accident that credit cards are so small and thin. I suspect that if credit card issuers could grease them up a bit, so that they slipped out of your pocket that much easier, they would do that too.

Credit card issuers do not want you to think about the money you are borrowing when you use your card. Studies have shown that people spend more money in a store when they use a credit card than when they have to pay with cash.

"(I)f people harbor a suspicion that they bought more impulsively because their credit cards make such buying easy, they were right. ... 'Plastic cards have an **anesthetizing effect***,' speculates Stephen M. Pollan, the writer and financial adviser. 'They allow people to temporarily ignore the question of whether they can really afford something or not.'"*

A Piece of the Action: How the Middle Class Joined the Money Class, Joseph Nocera

Watch for warning signs that you are incurring too much debt.

Many financial writers and commentators recommend watching out for **warning signs** that you are over-using your credit cards.

Here are some of the common warning signs:

1. You resist opening your credit card bills.

2. You need more than 20% of your after-tax income to make debt payments.

3. You don't make more than the required monthly payment for months at a time.

4. You use your credit card without thinking about the fact that you are borrowing money.

If you want to survive and succeed in the 21st century, train yourself to borrow and use debt responsibly.

9

Protect yourself against credit card fraud.

Credit card fraud occurs when someone illegally obtains and uses your credit card number. A related crime is identity theft when someone obtains personal information (e.g. your social security number) and uses that information to spend or borrow in your name, sometimes obtaining a credit card in your name. Credit card fraud is a big problem – costing lenders billions of dollars a year and costing consumers millions of hours disputing and correcting incorrect charges. To protect yourself against credit card fraud:

Do: Keep a record of your account numbers in a secure place, destroy carbons of credit card transactions, save receipts to compare against bills, notify card companies in advance of a change of your address.

Don't: Lend your card to anyone, give your credit card number over a cell phone, sign a receipt which has any blank spaces, give your account number to a vendor you are unsure about.

If you lose your card, call your credit card issuer immediately. Most companies have "24-7" emergency numbers. **Your maximum exposure for unlawful charges against your card is $50/card.**

For an excellent resource on consumer fraud and identity theft, see:

www.ftc.gov/

10

Keep up your FICO score.

There are a ton of writers and online commentators who offer advice about how to keep up your FICO score. The Fair Isaacs company itself tells you its most important criteria – the two biggies being: (1) How you pay your existing debt, and (2) How much debt you have against your total borrowing power.

Here are some of the tips from financial writers (see the bibliography for books on maximizing your score):

1. Make all your payments on time … DUH.

2. Don't close cards – you can choose not to use them, but by closing them you reduce your total borrowing power and thereby increase your debt-to-available-debt ratio. To prevent your card company from closing a card that you are not using, use it occasionally for small purchases.

3. If you feel you need to close cards (to stop from using them), close those you got most recently. FICO likes to see longevity in borrowing relationships.

4. As a young adult, consider temporarily "piggybacking" on a parent's card (as an authorized user). The new FICO formula that takes effect in 2009 will give you a credit score tied to your parents' credit history. (If your parent has a low FICO score, ignore this point!)

Be a comparative shopper.

Even in these times, when credit card companies are pulling back on offerings, there are many choices for credit cards, especially if you have decent credit.

Go online and compare cards. Here are a couple of good sites for credit card shopping:

www.bankrate.com
www.creditcards.com
www.cardratings.com

Sign on to a couple of the online credit card forums where you can ask people about their experience with a particular card or credit card issuer.

In selecting a card, consider how you are going to be using it. If you are going to be paying off your balance every month, then focus less on the APR, and more on rebates and rewards offerings. If you are looking to use your card to consolidate debt and transfer balances from other cards, look for a low introductory rate with the longest possible introductory period.

Finally, read all the snail mail and e-mail offers you receive. Card issuers have different objectives at different times, and sometimes you can find a good deal in snail mail or e-mail marketing offers.

Don't be sucked in by rebate or reward programs.

Curtis Arnold, founder of www.cardratings.com and author of *How to Use Credit Cards to Your Advantage,* advises that people who are going to be carrying a balance not even consider rewards offerings.

Credit card companies are not offering you rebates and rewards because they like you. They are doing this to get you to use their more expensive card. In addition, card companies have found that people use these cards to a greater degree than other cards. Credit card companies want to encourage card use even when they do not earn interest. That is because the merchants who accept credit cards also pay the card company a fee – usually about 2% of the purchase.

In other words, the credit card companies make money "coming and going."

If you are a person who never carries a balance, you might want to read the chapter in Arnold's book "*Show Me the Money!*" where he outlines strategies for maximizing rewards or rebates.

By the way, 85% of U.S. households with credit cards have at least one reward card.

Credit card issuers do not want to lose your business.

Credit card issuers want to make money, and that means they need to issue cards and maintain credit card relationships. Although they may presently be cutting back on offerings and limits and raising rates, they still need customers.

So, if your credit card company does something that you do not like, e.g. hits you with a late fee when you have never been late before, don't hesitate to pick up the phone and ask them to waive the fee.

If you have been a decent customer, it will cost the credit card issuer more money to replace you with another decent customer than it will to eliminate the fee. I suggest being very polite but making the point that you are prepared to close your card (bluffing is not illegal), and transfer your balance to another card if the fee is not waived.

"I would like to speak with a supervisor...."

Learn the strategies for reducing debt.

If you do find yourself in a credit card hole (like Billy and Beth), do not lose hope. There are many approaches to reducing that debt, short of bankruptcy or some other extreme measure. Here are some of them:

1. Call your credit card issuer. Explain your situation. Ask for a reduction of your interest rate, even if on a temporary basis.

2. Look for balance transfer opportunities at low introductory rates.

3. If there is any way you can, pay more than your minimum payment.

4. Sell something and use it to pay down debt.

5. If you feel unable to handle your debts, consider going to an advisor to develop what is usually called a Debt Management Plan. This is a program where a third-party negotiates with your credit card companies on your behalf. You make one payment a month (to the third party) who then pays your card company. The card companies pay the third party some portion of your monthly payment. The key is to find a reputable advisor. We recommend starting at the National Foundation for Credit Counseling (www.nfcc.org/).

— 15 —

Take personal responsibility.

The credit card world is like a big game. The credit card issuer wants to take money out of your pockets and put it into theirs. But, with minor exceptions (predatory lending), they are not doing so illegally. They may be giving you a shovel and allowing you to dig a hole for yourself, but they are not forcing you to dig.

You have the real power in the relationship. Ultimately, it's your choice whether the winner of the credit card game is YOU or, the card company. You are running the show. You can use the card responsibly. You can take advantage of its conven- ience, its float, its rebate and rewards programs. Don't look for excuses (yes, the credit card companies are tricky and their marketing is seductive). Look for the strength and knowledge to use cards to your advantage.

By the way, there are a lot of credit card "success stories." It is in fact rumored that Larry Brin and Sergei Paige started Google by using their credit cards to finance their start-up company's computers.

"I think we should call ourselves 'Google'."

"Are you nuts? What kind of name is 'Google'? That will never catch on."

CONCLUSION

Sir Francis Bacon said that "knowledge is power."

Here is what I hope you have learned:

1. The credit card companies are not your friend. They are out to make money off of you.

2. Still, you can educate yourself and not only protect yourself from making credit card mistakes but also take advantage of the conveniences that credit cards offer.

3. Understanding how to deal with credit cards is not brain surgery. With effort and time you can learn how to prevail against the credit card company forays.

We at **The Skinny On™** hope that you have enjoyed our book. As always, we would love to hear from you.

With warm regards,

Jim Randel
jrandel@randmediaco.com

AUTHOR'S BIO

BIBLIOGRAPHY

51 Ways to Save Hundreds on Loans and Credit Cards, S. Smith (FDIC 2007)

101 Tips for Legally Improving Your Credit Score, Manuel Braschi (e-book, 2008)

A Piece of the Action: How the Middle Class Joined the Money Class, Joseph Nocera (Simon & Schuster, 1994)

Credit Arbitrage, Joseph Morse (Code Publishing, 2007)

Credit Card Nation: The Consequences of America's Addiction to Debt, Robert Manning (Perseus, 2000)

Credit Scores & Credit Reports: How the System Really Works, What You Can Do, Evan Hendricks (Privacy Times, 2007)

Debt Cures "They" Don't Want You to Know About, Kevin Trudeau (Equity Press, 2008)

Fighting Fire with Fire: Charging Your Way out of Credit Card Debt, Bob Donnelly (Author House, 2007

Forever in Your Debt: Escaping Credit Card Hell, Harvey Z. Warren (2007)

How You Can Profit from Credit Cards, Curtis Arnold (FT Press, 2008)

Maxed Out: Hard Times in the Age of Easy Credit, James Scurlock (Scriber, 2007)

Paying with Plastic: The Digital Revolution in Buying and Borrowing, Evans and Schmalensee (MIT Press, 2005)

Personal Finance for Dummies, Eric Tyson (Wiley, 2006)

Start Late, Finish Rich, David Bach (Broadway Books, 2006)

Talk Your Way Out of Credit Card Debt, Scott Bilker (Press One Publishing, 2003)

The Automatic Millionaire, David Bach (Broadway Books, 2004)

The Credit Card Guidebook, Hardekopf and Oldshue (Hampton, 2008)

Secrets of the Millionaire Mind, T. Harv Eker (Harper, 2005)

Suze Orman's 2009 Action Plan, Suze Orman (Spiegel & Grau, 2009)

The Millionaire Zone, Jennifer Openshaw (Hyperion, 2007)

The 9 Steps to Financial Freedom, Suze Orman (Three River Press, 2006)

The Total Money Makeover, Dave Ramsey (Thomas Nelson, 2007)

The Wall Street Journal Personal Finance Book, Jeff Opdyke (Three River Press, 2006)

You're Broke Because You Want to Be, Larry Winget (Gotham Books, 2008)

Your Credit Score, Liz Pulliam Weston (Pearson, 2007)

Zero Debt for College Grads, Lynnette Khalfani (Kaplan, 2007)

And Hundreds of Online Articles, Comments and Blogs and Phone Calls to Experts

GLOSSARY

Allocation: How you payments are attributed.

Annual Percentage Rate (APR): the interest you are paying on your balance. Reminder: you can have different APR's. For example, if you have a low-interest introductory card and use that card to obtain money from your credit card company, the APR on the cash advance will not be the same as the introductory rate APR.

Average Daily Balance: if you carry a balance, your card company will charge you interest on that balance. They way they calculate that interest is by multiplying your daily interest rate (APR/365) against your balance on every day during your billing cycle.

Balance: that portion of your credit card bill you do not pay off monthly.

Balance Transfer Card: a card onto which you can transfer debt from another card or cards.

Cash Advance: money you can receive from your credit card company.

Credit Limit or Line: the total amount you can charge against your card.

Float: when your usage of the credit card company's money is free. For example, let's say you make a purchase on January 1 and receive your bill on January 20 and don't have to pay that bill until February 7. During the period between January 1 and February 7, you are considered to have a float (free usage) of the credit card company's money.

Grace Period: the time you have been receiving and paying your bill.

Interest: what you are paying your credit card company on the money they loan you.

Late Fee: big ugly expense for paying your bill late – even one day.

Over-the-Limit Fee: a charge when your total charges exceed your Credit Limit.

Rebate or Reward Card: based on your usage you get cash back or points to use for other purchases.

Revolver: a credit card holder who carries a balance month after month.

ANSWERS TO QUIZ ON PANEL 189:

1) E
2) H
3) K
4) N
5) T
6) P
7) A
8) O
9) C
10) M
11) F
12) Q
13) D
14) S
15) R
16) G
17) B
18) J
19) I
20) L